The Day the Lion Roars

Jamin Denslow

To Carolyn & Reese

Agape' Love

Jamin Denslow
(Jack)

TO SOW THE FALLOW SOIL

Winston-Derek Publishers, Inc.
Pennywell Drive—Post Office Box 90883
Nashville, Tennessee 37209

Copyright 1987 by Winston-Derek Publishers, Inc.

First printing

PUBLISHED BY WINSTON-DEREK PUBLISHERS, INC.
Nashville, Tennessee 37205

Library of Congress Catalog Card No: 86-40284
ISBN 1-55523-029-6

Printed in the United States of America

Introduction

I dedicate this book to truth and to the God of truth that I shall represent by the Hebrew Tetragrammaton, יהוה, the Hebrew Masoretic text rendering, Yᵉho•wah, or the Latin equivalent, Jehovah. I further give recognition to our King, Jesus Christ, who manifested these truths and sealed them in our hearts with his own blood.

For the past seventeen centuries, Christianity was gradually altered by traditions and fused with the thoughts of Greek philosophers. Greek terminology was translated into Latin, and Latin into modern languages—the original meaning being obscured or disguised and the original issues forgotten.

We are living in the end result of such transformation. Ideas of prophecy have been exchanged throughout each century. However, with the basic traditional concepts accepted as fact, modern day writers in the realm of Christendom study each political and revolutionary experience and search the Scriptures in an effort to apply them to these historical incidents. They have misapplied prophecy and have even gone "beyond the things written" in order to establish their own credentials.

I pray, as you approach the following chapters, you, the reader, will become as "little children," open-minded, meek and teachable. I will use twenty-eight translations so that you will discern the "truth," by comparison, "that will set you free" (John 8:32).

Contents

Chapter 1
Translation or Connotation

. . . seeking to establish their own,
they did not submit to God's righteousness.
Romans 10:3

Since the Bible is the chief source of Christian faith, wisdom and understanding are important as to whether it is an accurate translation or a connotation of man's opinion. It is important to know the difference. Failure to do so constitutes an obstacle in studying the unfolding purposes of God through prophecy. Another common obstruction is bibliolatry, or the feeling that the Bible is only used in solemn circumstances—a book of mysterious powers. Too many religious leaders have a counterfeit zeal and guard the sanctity of the Bible, failing to open the treasures to the people.

The most dangerous fallacy, and one with which this book deals, is the use of its symbolism, through seeming coincidences, to attest to the fulfillment of Biblical prophecy in the events surrounding us. A sin committed by many interpreters of the Bible is their indiscriminate use of "proof texts" in dogmatic assertions. It creates what I refer to as "faith in faith," i.e., faith in what an individual claims is true rather than what God inspires.

This act of assertion is founded on traditions. Traditions are opinions, doctrines or practices handed down from age to age, many times without being committed to writing. Paul speaks of beneficial traditions or the ones received directly from Jesus Christ [1 Corinthians 11:2]. However, the traditions about which we are concerned present a danger of inaccuracy, or they are those contrary to the

Word of God. Let's now consider the painstaking task of Bible translating.

Hebrew Scriptures

The Hebrew alphabet was composed of twenty-two consonants with some combinations extending it to twenty-eight sounds. Since there were no vowels, the pronunciation was handed down by those responsible for reading the Law, Prophets and Psalms.

When the Grecian world power defeated the Persian dynasty in 332 B.C., they also captured the Jews. On the north shore of Egypt, there sprang up the city of Alexandria, named for the great conqueror. It became a center for Greek culture and learning. An effort was made to translate the Jewish Law into Greek. Seventy scholars undertook the task; and in a short time, they produced what is known as the Septuagint Bible, the word literally meaning, "seventy."

דברי הימים ב יב יג

8 כִּי יִהְיוּ־לוֹ לַעֲבָדִים וְיֵדְעוּ עֲבוֹדָתִי
9 וַעֲבוֹדַת מַמְלְכוֹת הָאֲרָצוֹת : וַיַּעַל
שִׁישַׁק מֶלֶךְ־מִצְרַיִם עַל־יְרוּשָׁלַםִ וַיִּקַּח
אֶת־אֹצְרוֹת בֵּית־יְהוָֹה וְאֶת־אֹצְרוֹת בֵּית
הַמֶּלֶךְ אֶת־הַכֹּל לָקָח וַיִּקַּח אֶת־מָגִנֵּי
10 הַזָּהָב אֲשֶׁר עָשָׂה שְׁלֹמֹה : וַיַּעַשׂ
הַמֶּלֶךְ רְחַבְעָם תַּחְתֵּיהֶם מָגִנֵּי נְחֹשֶׁת
וְהִפְקִיד עַל־יַד שָׂרֵי הָרָצִים הַשֹּׁמְרִים
11 פֶּתַח בֵּית הַמֶּלֶךְ : וַיְהִי מִדֵּי־בוֹא
הַמֶּלֶךְ בֵּית יְהוָֹה בָּאוּ הָרָצִים וּנְשָׂאוּם
12 וֶהֱשִׁיבוּם אֶל־תָּא הָרָצִים : וּבְהִכָּנְעוֹ
שָׁב מִמֶּנּוּ אַף יְהוָֹה וְלֹא לְהַשְׁחִית לְכָלָה
13 וְגַם בִּיהוּדָה הָיָה דְּבָרִים טוֹבִים : וַיִּתְחַזֵּק הַמֶּלֶךְ רְחַבְעָם
בִּירוּשָׁלַםִ וַיִּמְלֹךְ כִּי בֶן־אַרְבָּעִים וְאַחַת
שָׁנָה רְחַבְעָם בְּמָלְכוֹ וּשְׁבַע עֶשְׂרֵה שָׁנָה ׀

ΠΑΡΑΛΕΙΠΟΜΕΝΩΝ Β΄, ιβ΄, ιγ΄.

8 "Οτι ἔσονται εἰς παῖδας, καὶ γνώσονται τὴν δουλείαν μου καὶ τὴν δουλείαν τῆς βασιλείας τῆς γῆς. 9 Καὶ ἀνέβη Σουσακὶμ βασιλεὺς Αἰγύπτου ἐπὶ Ἱερουσαλήμ, καὶ ἔλαβε τοὺς θησαυροὺς τοὺς ἐν οἴκῳ Κυρίου καὶ τοὺς θησαυροὺς τοὺς ἐν οἴκῳ τοῦ βασιλέως, τὰ πάντα ἔλαβε· καὶ ἔλαβε τοὺς θυρεοὺς τοὺς χρυσοῦς οὓς ἐποίησε Σαλωμών. 10 Καὶ ἐποίησεν ὁ βασιλεὺς Ῥοβοὰμ θυρεοὺς χαλκοῦς ἀντ᾽ αὐτῶν· καὶ κατέστησεν ἐπ᾽ αὐτὸν Σουσακὶμ ἄρχοντας παρατρεχόντων τοὺς φυλάσσοντας τὸν πυλῶνα τοῦ βασιλέως. 11 Καὶ ἐγίνετο ἐν τῷ εἰσελθεῖν τὸν βασιλέα εἰς οἶκον Κυρίου, εἰσεπορεύοντο οἱ φυλάσσοντες καὶ οἱ παρατρέχοντες καὶ οἱ ἐπιστρέφοντες εἰς ἀπάντησιν τῶν παρατρεχόντων. 12 Καὶ ἐν τῷ ἐντραπῆναι αὐτὸν ἀπεστράφη ἀπ᾽ αὐτοῦ ὀργὴ Κυρίου, καὶ οὐκ εἰς καταφθορὰν εἰς τέλος· καὶ γὰρ ἐν Ἰούδᾳ ἦσαν λόγοι ἀγαθοί. 13 Καὶ κατίσχυσεν ὁ βασιλεὺς Ῥοβοὰμ ἐν Ἱερουσαλὴμ

2

Jews, called Massoretes, were dissatisfied with the Sacred Scriptures being spoken in Greek and were in fear that the original language would cease to exist. They retained the Hebrew Scriptures and invented vowel signs which they sprinkled in among those consonants. These two ancient texts of the Old Testament became the most important manuscripts, not only to scholars, but to all believers in Christianity. They were the Bibles of Jesus and the early Christians. There is little doubt as to the general accuracy of the Hebrew renditions.

Christian Greek Scriptures

With the Christian Greek Scriptures, more commonly called the New Testament, the situation is quite different. The teachings were carried abroad orally, especially by impetuous Peter and energetic Paul. From various locations there were letters of warning, of encouragement, and of exhortation sent to scattered congregations. These letters were the beginning of Christian literature. Near the close of the second century, a list of New Testament books, almost complete, was compiled.

The major threat came from the foretold apostasy that would arise from those professing to be Christians. The early congregation was, at first, very simple. Congregations met in homes, and no distinction between laymen and clergy was recognized. Gradually, under the influence of the pagan religious beliefs, the ritual of Christianity increased to such a stage of complexity that a professional priesthood seemed to become necessary. The Kingdom of God, which was the main teaching of Jesus, played a small part in the Christian creeds. In time, there was a development that adversely affected the influence of the Bible in the lives of those who professed faith in it. The teachings of the Roman Church were placed on the same level as the Scriptures. Ceremonies and rituals were stressed, and the people no longer viewed the reading of the Bible to be of any importance. The Bible was to remain in Latin, now a dead language. Even many of the priests and ministers could no longer read Latin.

The sixteenth century brought about a drastic change. The critical study of the Holy Scriptures during the great revival of Bible scholars raised many questions and doubts. It became evident that many doctrines and practices resting upon traditions were exposed and in jeopardy. It also questioned the authority of the papal administration.

The difficulty and challenges that now faced these scholars in translating the Greek Scriptures proved to be demanding. Languages are very complex and differ from each other in grammar, sentence structure and vocabulary. Although Greek was nearly universally known during the time of Christ and became the dialect common to all, problems were evident. The alphabet was borrowed from the Semites and contains twenty-four characters; however, capital letters and punctuations are not utilized, and the use of other grammatical techniques such as the definite article [the], cases, active and passive voices, accent marks, syllable and breathing marks are unique to the language. This allows for interpretation or connotation at the whim of the translator and only can be proven otherwise by carefully "examining the Scriptures as to whether these things are so" (Acts 17:11).

The "Received Text"

The development of the printing press provides a remarkable history of achievement. It permitted the making of books in quantity and more cheaply. Rather than have the Scriptures only in the Latin translations, long used in the Roman Church, scholars began to clamor for copies in other languages. Berthold Ruppel is usually credited with the introduction of printing into Switzerland in 1468. The most famous and learned printer in Swiss history was Joannes Froben. With him was associated the Dutch scholar,

Desiderius Erasmus. Herbert Dennett's *Graphic Guide to Modern Versions of the New Testament* explains the circumstances surrounding his well-known *Received Text*.

> "The task, however, was undertaken at short notice, and executed in haste. Erasmus used but half a dozen manuscripts, only one of which was moderately old and reliable. None of his manuscripts contained the whole of the New Testament, and some verses which were not in any of them were actually retranslated by Erasmus into Greek from the Latin. This published text was later revised with the help of a few further manuscripts, but the result affected the work but little."

This incident in history is significant to us because many translations were made using the *Received Text* as reference. Sir Frederic Kenyon in his, *Our Bible and the Ancient Manuscript*, noted this:

> "The result is that the text accepted in the sixteenth and seventeenth centuries, to which we have clung from the natural reluctance to change the words which we have learnt as those of the Word of God, is, in truth, full of inaccuracies, many of which can be corrected with absolute certainty from the vastly wider material which is at our disposal today."

The availability of ancient Greek manuscripts during the sixteenth and seventeenth centuries were few in number. As Greek scholars became acquainted with older and more accurate manuscripts, they noticed the many flaws. In fact, even after it was edited four additional times since it was first published in 1516, the last edition of 1535 still contained nearly 10,000 errors of translation. However, scholars were in bondage to the Erasmian-oriented *Received Text* and rather than change the text, they would publish their findings in introductions, margins and foot-notes of editions.

I would like to refer back to a statement I made pre-viously in this chapter. It read, "It became evident that many doctrines and practices resting upon traditions were exposed." Evidences of two major acts of connotation are about to unfold.

First, the Protestant Reformation did not accomplish the return to pure doctrine and service to God. The ninety-five theses that Martin Luther nailed to the church door at Wittenburg, Germany, were primarily in protest to the prac-tices of selling indulgences, i.e., a way one could shorten the stay of a relative or friend in purgatory. Some even bought forgiveness of sins.

Malachi Martin in his book, *Decline and Fall of the Roman Catholic Church*, explains that Pope Leo X had a love for money and that he was obsessed with it. He allowed Prince Albert to sell a special inventory of indul-gences. He even stated the amount required from persons from different stations in life. He further states:

> "To enhance his position as source of mercy for the faithful suffering in Purgatory, Prince Albert had something special, his collection of relics [all, of course, fraudulent]: a wisp of straw from the manger, four hairs from the Virgin's head, fourteen pieces of her clothing, a strand of Christ's beard, a nail from the cross, a little over 19,093 sacred bone parts of saints. For venerating all this and a pay-ment, anyone could shorten the stay of any close friend or relative in Purgatory."

While some of the views held by Luther were more in line with the Scriptures, he did not go far enough. He retained many traditional doctrines and beliefs without any consideration that they may be false. This brought about the second connotation. New translations had to be altered to conform to unscriptural teachings.

King James or Authorized Version

There were many translations made from the *Received Text*. Since this publication is for the expressed purpose of presenting true prophecy and the fact that "God cannot lie," we will only mention translations that have direct effect on the believing ranks of Christianity. Remember, it is essential that we use good discernment in assessing Bible translations to be sure we are reading a faithful and accurate reflection of the original writings.

There are two types of translations: a literal rendition and a paraphrase. The first one clings primarily to the original text or as much as idioms and word choice will allow. The paraphrase is a free translation in which the translator seeks to express the thoughts of the writer *as he may have interpreted them*. Bibles which have been paraphrased can be colorful and easy to read because they are expressed in the language of the day. However, caution should be exercised in taking everything one reads as completely reliable and accurate. The literal translation should be the most accurate, but as one will discern from the following inquiry, all translations are affected when the approach is influenced by a preconceived belief.

The King James Version is accepted by more people than any other single Bible translation. To really know a translation, you must first know why it was written. Remember, we read the Bible to learn the will of God and not to be entertained by the style and poetic fervor of archaic English.

King James VI was King of Scotland in 1567. In 1603, his cousin Elizabeth I died, and he assumed the role of King James I of both England and Scotland. He always believed in the "divine right of kings," i.e., the King's right to rule came directly from God. This self-given authority inspired him to sponsor the third "authorized" version, the first two being the *Great Bible* and the *Bishops' Bible*.

This "authorized" version was to be translated from the oldest mss; but some fifty scholars altered existing translations. It finally emerged in 1611. No one reads the version in its original form. Today, we are in the ninth edition or change. From 1611 to 1613, the second edition introduced three hundred twenty-eight unauthorized changes and additions. In the eighteenth century, major changes were made with the addition of nearly 32,000 references including punctuations and the use of capitals. In 1856, the American Bible Society found nearly 24,000 variations in six different editions. Today, the King James Version still has nearly 2,000 errors of translation, including additions, deletions, and incorrect usage of vocabulary and punctuations. We will illustrate the following variations using the King James Bible as compared with the Vatican manuscript of the fourth century. The text, John 1:1.

King James

"In the beginning was the Word, and the Word was with God, and the Word was God."

Vatican Ms

1 Ἐν ἀρχῇ ἦν ὁ λόγος, καὶ ὁ λόγος
  In beginning was the Word, and the Word
ἦν πρὸς τὸν θεόν, καὶ θεὸς ἦν ὁ λόγος.
was toward the God, and god was the Word.
2 Οὗτος ἦν ἐν ἀρχῇ πρὸς τὸν θεόν.
  This (one) was in beginning toward the God.

Why the difference in the use of the word, God or god? The first use of the "Word" is not the same as the second. The definite article "the" [ho] appears before the first one. Because of this, the translator, James Moffatt, translates the last part of the verse as, "The Word was divine." The second noun is referred to as "anarthrous," meaning, used without the article. When a Greek noun does not have the article in front of it, it becomes rather a description. In this case, *a god* or *divine*.

Another point of consideration is that the Word was with the God. A person who is *with* someone is not the same as the one he is with. Further support of this is that the first use of the word God is literally translated from Theon, and is in the accusative case, while the second use is Theos, in the nominative case. It is definitely speaking of two, distinct personalities, not one and the same.

Remember, we are not discussing doctrine. Whether one believes in a triune God or a monolistic form should not be the deciding criteria for translating this text, especially in light of what John further said in verse 18. It reads that "No man has seen God at any time; the only begotten *god* who is in the bosom position with the Father is the one that has explained him" (John. 1:18).

It is interesting to note that Matthew and Luke spoke of the birth of Jesus during the reign of Caesar Augustus. John's introduction takes us to the beginning of creation. To receive the full realization of this, scientists claim that the universe is approximately 20 billion years old. John's application in the opening verse was long before that time since it isn't inclusive of the creation of spiritual creatures. What magnitude!

Consider Philippians 2:5, 6.

King James

"Let this mind be in you which was also in Christ Jesus: who being in the form of God, thought it not robbery to be equal with God."

Vatican Ms

5 τοῦτο φρονεῖτε ἐν ὑμῖν ὃ καὶ
This be you minding in you which also
ἐν Χριστῷ Ἰησοῦ, 6 ὃς ἐν μορφῇ θεοῦ
in Christ Jesus, who in form of God
ὑπάρχων οὐχ ἁρπαγμὸν ἡγήσατο τὸ εἶναι
existing not snatching he considered the to be
ἴσα θεῷ,
equal (things) to God,

John 1:1 could be considered a judgmental decision, but the text just sighted indicates an intent to deceive. It speaks of humility on the part of the Christ and that, although he was a mighty spirit, gave no consideration of equality as Satan tried to make himself like God. The trouble with those translations that try to make it appear that Jesus had equality with God in heaven is that they insert the pronoun "it" into the text.

Today, this inaccurate rendition is well known to Bible scholars. Still, the same intent of deception is being practiced by newer translations such as the paraphrase edition of *The Living Bible* and one to recently crowd the marketplace entitled, *The Book*.

Since the Greek language uses no punctuation, it became evident that personal selection would be made. Notice how proper punctuations can bring new meaning to Luke 23:43.

King James   Vatican Ms

"And Jesus said unto him, Verily I say unto Thee, Today shalt thou be with me in paradise."

43 καὶ	εἶπεν		
And	he said		
αὐτῷ 'Αμήν	σοι	λέγω,	σήμερον μετ'
to him Amen	to you	I am saying	today with
ἐμοῦ ἔση	ἐν	τῷ	παραδείσῳ.
me you will be	in	the	Paradise.

In the King James version, the comma being placed before the word "today" makes it appear that Jesus told the evildoer that he would be in paradise that very same day. However, this would have been impossible since Jesus was resurrected on the third day from his death. Since the Apostle John at Revelation, chapter 12, speaks of God's Kingdom as being in the future, it should have directed the translator to reconsider his decision.

What Jesus was saying was that when the Kingdom by Christ is established according to God's timetable, the evildoer can expect to be resurrected into the paradisiacal promise.

I would like to reiterate again that this book is not intended to dispute doctrine, but rather it is making an effort to read the Word of God as the writer clarifies his position. On many occasions, it is necessary to study the conditions that exist at the time of writing to grasp the full meaning. One such case is found at Mark 9:47.

King James   Vatican Ms

"And if thine eye offend thee, Pluck it out: it is better for thee to enter into the Kingdom of God with one eye, than have two eyes to be cast into hell fire."

47 καὶ	ἐὰν	ὁ	ὀφθαλμός	σου
And	if ever	the	eye	of you
σκανδαλίζη		σε,	ἔκβαλε	αὐτόν·
may be stumbling		you,	throw out	it;
καλόν σέ	ἐστιν	μονόφθαλμον	εἰσελθεῖν	εἰς
fine you	it is	one-eyed	to enter	into
τὴν βασιλείαν	τοῦ	θεοῦ	ἢ δύο ὀφθαλμοὺς	
the kingdom	of the	God	than two eyes	
ἔχοντα	βληθῆναι	εἰς	γέενναν,	
having	to be thrown	into	Gehenna,	

The fourth century manuscript uses the term, "Gehenna." It is found twelve times in the Christian Greek Scriptures. The New Bible Commentary says:

> "Gehenna was the Hellenized form of the name of the valley of Hinnon at Jerusalem in which fires were kept constantly burning to consume the refuse of the city. This is a powerful picture of final destruction."

There are no texts that associate Gehenna with suffering or conscious existence after death. The confusion comes when the word is substituted with "hell fire." "Hell" is an English terminology meaning "to conceal" and was not known by the early Christians. However, from the sixteenth century on, translators have carelessly used the term to prove previously made convictions.

During the reign of King Josiah, idolatry ran rampant and the valley of Hinnon was used for human sacrifices to Baal. Due to Israel's last good king, it became a place for the disposal of garbage including carcasses of dead animals and even criminals that were thought too evil to be saved, but nothing alive. Since it was located just south and southwest of Jerusalem, the fire was increased in intensity by the addition of sulphur to allow the stench to rise, thus avoiding the city. Where the fire did not reach, worms would breed, consuming anything not destroyed by the fire. Jesus was illustrating, not eternal torment as depicted by the term "hell fire," but total destruction. *The Revised Standard Bible,* at 2 Thessalonians 1:7-9, sums it up precisely:

> " . . . and to grant rest with us to you who are afflicted, when the Lord Jesus is revealed from heaven with his mighty angels in a flaming fire, inflicting vengeance upon those who do not know God and upon those who do not obey the Gospel of our Lord Jesus. They shall suffer the punishment

11

of ETERNAL DESTRUCTION and exclusion from the presence of the Lord."

For your edification, I will sight three other examples of additions that have not been revealed as spurious:

Mark 16:9-20, speaks of signs that would follow God's followers down through the ages, such as handling of serpents, drinking poisons, and the laying on of hands for the purpose of healing. This text does not rest on ancient authority; in fact, it is doubtful that it was even written by Mark.

John 8:1-11, speaks of the adulterous woman that was forgiven by Christ and is used quite frequently in Hollywood productions. The text cannot be found in any known reliable manuscript.

1 John 5:7, speaks of the Father, Son and Holy Ghost as one, and according to the Catholic publication, *New Testament Problems*, admits to the addition of the text in the sixteenth century.

This chapter on "Translation or Connotation" is necessary to show how imperfect man will feign ignorance of a wrong; however, he will use it to his own satisfaction. The following chapters will convey this attempt in prophecy.

Chapter 2
Test By Fire

... and thus we have gained fresh
confirmation of the prophetic word.

2 Peter 1:19

Since men have been upon earth, their minds have been constantly assaulted for capture. Ideas conveyed to the minds of men are more powerful than merely physical forces. It is vital that we ascertain whether the Bible contains the truth of God's Word or simply good human philosophy. What makes this examination so much more important in all aspects is the fact that we are living in the day of judgement. The extreme agitation in world governments is a prerequisite to the destruction that threatens the human race. If the Bible is what it claims to be, it shouldn't be difficult to prove the infallibility of its prophetic word.

A Doctor's Viewpoint

To scrutinize the Scriptures with a magnification of the mind's eye will open an entirely new respect for the Word of God. The doctor, here mentioned, is Luke, a dedicated follower of Jesus Christ and one who has contributed much to the prophetic plan of our day. He was well educated, which is confirmed by his fluent style of writing, but most important to this observation was his use of medical expressions.

In Jesus' parable of the good Samaritan, Luke described the exact procedure used by physicians of his day for the treatment of lacerations and contusions. The man fell among robbers who both stripped him and, as the original text asserts, "inflicted blows" so that he was left half dead.

His treatment was to "bound up his wounds, pouring oil and wine upon them" (Luke 10:29-37).

When Jesus was arrested, the accounts of Matthew and Mark indicate that Peter "cut off Malchus' ear"; however, Luke specifically states it was his "right ear" (Luke 22:50, 51).

Luke reported that Peter's mother-in-law "was distressed with a high fever" (Luke 4:38, 39).

No other writer employed this terminology. Observe the writings of Luke and confirm the fact that the Bible is accurate in every respect.

Medically Sound

The Mosaic Law, given to the nation of Israel, proves the inspirational backing of a superior mind. It was written nearly 3500 years ago, and it was to safeguard the health and welfare of the people. Eventually, the great civilizations surrounding Israel, with implications directed primarily to Egypt, realized the benefits derived from these principles and incorporated them into their own concepts for eliminating disease (Exodus 15:26).

A regulation that proved to be good for the people was the matter of dealing with human excrement. Deuteronomy 23:12, 13 minces no words as to the treatment. It reads, "You must have a latrine outside the camp, and go out to this; and you must have a mattock among your equipment, and with this mattock, when you go outside to ease yourself, you must dig a hole and cover your excrement." It's ironic that the continent of Europe had no sound sanitary system during the nineteenth century. In fact, medical students just a century ago, after dissecting a corpse, entered hospital wards without necessary sanitary procedures. It resulted in the death of one out of eight patients. This epidemic could never have happened to the nation of Israel as long as they observed the laws of protection (Numbers 19:11-22).

God commanded Abraham that circumcision was to be

performed after the male child was eight days old. Today, physicians see the wisdom of this procedure because it was discovered that not until the fifth to the eighth day after birth is a normal amount of the blood-clotting element known as "vitamin K," and "prothrombin" evident in the blood stream.

Fever had been known as a sign of illness since the observation of Hippocrates. However, Moses recorded much about the subject more than a thousand years earlier (Leviticus 26:16).

What of the physiological composition of man? Does the Bible contain proof that he is the product of a creator? Many people are not aware that all substances found in the earth are in the make-up of man. Terms such as embryo, kidneys, heart, liver, intestines, ligaments, muscles, as well as the circulatory system, are used throughout the Scriptures. Quarantining was incorporated before a micro-organism was ever thought to exist. It bears out the recent discovery that civilization of a high order appeared suddenly and that language studies show the oldest tongue is the most complex. Clear indications have been made as to the wisdom of the Bible that was not shared by the world's wise men at the time it was recorded. Neither was this wisdom found in the ranks of the wise down through the ages until within a century and a half of our present day achievements.

Scientific Assertions

To primitive man, the planet was a flat disk with its surface separated by mountains, rivers and seas. The spherical form was asserted by Pythagoras and Aristotle; however, it was not firmly believed until after explorers sailed around the earth. The Bible was far ahead of this misconception of the universe when it stated, "Have you not understood how the earth was founded? He lives above the *circle* of the earth" (Isaiah 40:21, 22).

Scientists such as Newton, Einstein and Birkhoff were aware of the common fact that any unsupported body falls to the ground. The attempt to understand the laws of and the reason for this very ordinary observation of gravitation has resulted in the development of many theories. Although the law was intriguing to the inquiring mind, the most astounding puzzlement was the gravitational action that somehow upheld the order of the universe.

One common view in ancient mythology was that the earth was supported by elephants standing on a large sea turtle, which was described as a circular plate. The first book of maps had a picture of a man holding up the world. People began calling the book, *The Atlas Book*.

Did such a line of reasoning influence the Bible writers? The unsearchable Word of God states that "the northern skies he spreads o'er empty space, and hangs the earth on nothing" (Job 26:7).

In the beginning account of Genesis, a logical order of both animate and inanimate creations was recorded in chapter one. This prescribed arrangement is fully corroborated by geology and the operation of everything that exists. The mathematical odds against the ancient writers guessing this sequence is overwhelming.

The waters of the earth move continuously from the oceans to the air to the land, and back to the oceans. This endless circulation is called the water or hydrologic cycle. It has only been within the last century that scientists have fully understood this wondrous process of nature. However, King Solomon, nearly thirty centuries ago, summed it up simply as "all the rivers run into the sea; yet the sea is not full; unto the place from whence the rivers come, thither they return again" (Ecclesiastes 1:7).

The study of the heavens show it to be an expanding universe and the 100-inch telescope only verifies that it is still flying apart as the result of a creative explosion.

Science does not contradict or disprove the dimensions of the Bible. If anything, scientific research causes man to stand in awe before his omniscient Creator.

Rife Archaeology

Archaeology is still heralding the trumpet of discovery. The foundations of modern civilization are to be found in the heritage which ancient civilizations of the Mediterranean area have left for us. The Bible had played an important role in the ever conquest for knowledge. The historical and geographical locations have been in absolute harmony with the Scriptures.

Many historical names mentioned in the Bible were missing from non-Biblical histories as well as customs and religious practices. Authentication came to light when inscriptions and objects were unearthed.

To illustrate this point, consider the Hittite people and their empires. They were the earliest known inhabitants of what is now known as Turkey. They began to control the area about 1900 B.C. David had Uriah, the Hittite, killed in battle so that he could marry Uriah's wife, Bathsheba. The name appears many times in the Old Testament but is completely forgotten in secular history. In fact, their existence became extremely doubtful.

In 1871, archaeologists began to find references to them in Egyptian writings. Authentication to a greater extent came in 1906 when the German archaeologist, Hugo Winckler discovered the capital city (Genesis 23:1-20).

One of the more famous occurrences in the Bible, and one spoken of by Jesus Christ, is the destruction of Sodom and Gomorrah (Genesis 19:12-26). The cities were located in "the Low Plain of Siddim," known as the Dead Sea. Geologists, after examining the location, determined that volcanic action took place about 1900 B.C., and the remains became submerged. In The New York Times of April 29, 1960, the following report was made: "Find in Dead Sea

Linked to Sodom . . . Dr. Ralph E. Barney of Kansas City, MO, head of a four member expedition, told an interviewer of finding extensive underwater remnants of the civilization that flourished and languished 4,000 years ago. The evidence indicated that the cities of the once fertile plain had been engulfed after a levee collapsed in an earthquake." This confirms Genesis 19:27, 28, where it reads, "Rising early in the morning, Abraham went to the place where he had stood before Yahweh, and looking towards Sodom and Gomorrah, and across the plain, he saw smoke rising from the land, like smoke from a furnace."

Although these features give solid reasons for believing that the Bible is more than human origination, the most striking observation is the remarkable fulfillment of its prophecies or history written in advance.

Prophetic Patterns

Nothing is more peculiarly characteristic of the religion and history of Israel than the mission of the prophets and the exercise of their unique gifts. There were prophets of God that acted as messengers and a man dedicated to see his Lord's will done and sent forth to proclaim it. There was also a multitude of professional prophets who were trained to exercise prophetic functions and who practiced them as a profession, exciting themselves with music and wild dances. They were not divinely inspired, and some of them were directly opposed to the mind of Yahweh. It is important to observe the distinction between the two classes. The same caution should be exercised today because a vast amount of prophetic interpretation is a mere echo of popular cries. The true prophets were too often in opposition to popular trends and experienced physical and verbal persecution.

Seventy Heptads

From before the founding of the world, God spoke the first prophecy pertaining to a promised seed. He would be

18

called in the Hebrew tongue, the Messiah (Genesis 3:15). An unmistakable identification had to be provided since it means life or death on "The Day the Lion Roars."

The book, *Archaeology and Bible History,* by Professor J. P. Free, gives an estimation figure of 332 distinct prophecies that were fulfilled in Christ Jesus. He further states:

> "The chances of all these prophecies being fulfilled in one man are so overwhelmingly remote that it is strikingly demonstrated that they could in no wise be shrewd guesses of mere men."

First and foremost was the prophecy that would precisely become an indicator as to his appearance on earth. Daniel's prophecy of "Seventy Heptads" or "Seventy Weeks" discloses this truth.

Delusions

The significance of Gabriel's words to Daniel is not yet determined by Jewish commentators. In an effort to exert an explanation, some exegetes have deviously tampered with the text. Many non-Jewish translations render these words incorrectly and ultimately distort the meaning.

According to the "Holy Scriptures," as published by the Jewish Publication Society, the prophecy reads:

> "Seventy weeks are decreed upon thy people and upon thy holy city, to finish the transgression, and to make an end to sin, and to forgive iniquity, and to bring in everlasting righteousness, and to seal vision and prophet and to anoint the most holy place. Know therefore and discern, that from the going forth of the word to restore and to build Jerusalem unto one anointed, a prince, shall be seven weeks; [Ath•nahh] and for the threescore and two weeks, it shall be built again, with broad place and moat, but in troublous times. And after the three-

score and two weeks shall an anointed one be cut off, and be no more; and the people of a prince that shall come shall destroy the city and the sanctuary" (Daniel 9:24-26).

The Jewish commentators link the end of the first group of seven weeks, i.e., forty-nine years, to Cyrus the Great as the anointed one, and then assuming the second anointed one in verse 26 to be the high priest, Joshua. They could ascertain this after the Masoretes added to the Hebrew text at verse 25, an *Ath•nahh* or *stop*. This semicolon divided the number of weeks, whereas they should be considered as a composite figure of sixty-nine weeks. Likewise, the translation added the word *for* before the sixty-two weeks. This makes it appear that Jerusalem will be completely rebuilt at the end of this time or approximately toward the spring of 163 B.C.

On the other hand, modern day exploiters of prophetic hubbub apply the Scriptures to an anti-Christ. In his book, *The 1980's—Countdown to Armageddon,* Hal Lindsey heedlessly injects the term whenever it accommodates his fancy. In his chapter, "Up Against the Wall," he says, "In exchange for the European leader's protection and a guarantee of temple rights in old Jerusalem, Israel will sign the treaty and worship the Jewish false prophet as the messiah and the anti-Christ as God himself." From the last part of this prophecy, he once again strains the Scriptures to conceive a "seven year" tribulation. I will cover the erroneous significance of this in later chapters; however, it must be noted and remembered that there is no indicator that extends the prophecy beyond the following designated time period.

Eracity

Complete understanding of this prophetic identification is only possible if the beginning and length of the seventy weeks is completely understood.

Nehemiah records a decree that was issued by Artaxerxes, King of Persia. It was in the twentieth year of his reign and the month of Nisan. It was "to restore and to rebuild Jerusalem" (Nehemiah 1:1-3; 2:1-8). From the chronological records of King Xerxes I, the father of Artaxerxes, historical evidence indicates his rule began in 474 B.C.

The length of time is a matter of the Hebrew word, *shavuim* [masculine], meaning that it is not the normal cycle of seven days, but rather, seven years. With this thought in mind, many English translators render the text as "weeks of years." Therefore, sixty-nine weeks of years would figure to 483 years. Since the decree was given during the twentieth year of his reign, we commence counting from 455 B.C., in the month of Tishri, for a total of 483 years. We arrive at the year 29 A.D., or the year the Son of God became the "anointed one" according to Daniel.

The prophecy further states that after half of the seventieth week of years was completed, the "anointed one would be cut off." Sure enough, according to the time predicted, Jesus was put to death by his own people, and the "sacrifice and gift offering ceased." At the end of the seventieth week of years or 36 A.D., the first gentile, Cornelius, was anointed. The prophecy further discloses the destruction of Jerusalem in 70 A.D. by General Titus.

Think of the tremendous force exerted and capacity to exercise control that it demanded to bring about the fulfillment of a prophecy of such precision. It is now nearly 2,000 years since Jesus' death and foretold prophecies are still occurring in this time of the end.

Tyrian Siege

Tyre was an ancient and famous city of Phoenicia situated on the coast of the Mediterranean Sea. Its site was upon what was originally an island, and there was a city called "Old Tyre" on the mainland. It was one of the great commercial cities of antiquity, and its king, Hiram, formed and maintained a friendship with Israel without the friction of military power. Early in his reign, King David had made an arrangement with the people of Tyre and Sidon to build the palace in Jerusalem. Wood of cedar was furnished by the King, and the workers were repaid with wine and produce. This association was strictly commercial because the Tyrians continued to practice Baal worship.

Tyre's reputation of power spread throughout the territory, and then the time came when they exalted themselves even over the God of the nation of Israel (Isaiah 23:8, 9). Compare Isaiah with Ezekiel 28:2-5. Their defiance brought about a divine judgment of downfall.

Babylon, under the rule of Nebuchadnezzar, laid siege against Tyre. The attack lasted thirteen years, and the loss was great on both sides. The Scriptures indicate that the heads of the soldiers were "worn bald" from the friction of the helmets, and their shoulders, "smooth" from carrying construction materials to be used in their conquest. God used Nebuchadnezzar as his servant to punish mainland Tyre, but the siege was not enough to end its rapacious rule. They managed to build an island city, thought to be impregnable. Zechariah's prophecy of Tyre's restoration was written nearly *200 years before it was fulfilled* (Zechariah 9:3, 4).

When Alexander the Great entered Phoenicia after the battle of Issus, Sidon submitted to his rule, but Tyre in its pride resisted. The capture of this city by siege and storm was the most brilliant of all his military exploits. He succeeded in building a mole from the mainland to the isle on which the city stood. He mounted huge towers on ships, and even fought Tyrian divers under the water who tried to cut holes in the bottoms of the ships. Nearly 8,000 Tyrians were killed and some 32,000 sold in slavery. The rage of Alexander was so unyielding that he shoved the city into the sea and scraped the surface bare. This action was foretold in prophecy about 591 B.C. It was fulfilled in 332 B.C., *a time differential of over 250 years.*

Huge stones and fragments of the ancient city are found along the shore and partially submerged. Here, today, fishermen spread their nets (Ezekiel 26:4, 14). Prophecy is a governing factor in our lives, whether we want to admit to it or not. As Jesus said, "I have told you before it occurs, in order that, when it does occur, you may believe."

The Rose-Red City

The civilization of southern Transjordan and situated to the south of Palestine between the Dead Sea and the Gulf of 'Akaba, was recognized in the Bible as Se'la. Later, under the domination of the Nabataeans, the city was known as Petra, the rose-red city. It was one of the great cities of Edom. The city was a virtually impregnable, flat-topped mountain. Structures were carved in the soft, rose-red sandstone cliffs. It was accessible only by a ravine through which the river winds across the site. There was an abundant water supply from cisterns and a uniquely constructed aqueduct system. Obadiah vividly describes this spectacular sight of the Palestine area:

> "Your pride of heart had played you false, perched in your fastness of the rocks, you who built your home so high, thinking none could pull you down." (Obadiah 3).

The occupants of Edom, during practically the whole period of Biblical history, were the Bedouin tribes, descendants through Esau from Abraham. Jacob said of his son Esau that "by your sword you will live," and it proved to be true. Because of the revengeful attacks upon the Jews, their speedy destruction was foretold (Obadiah 10-12).

The inhabitants of the city showed no symptoms of concern. They failed to realize that their demise would come from the Chaldeans, once their confederates (Jeremiah 27:6).

In the year 602 B.C., according to prophecy, Nebuchadnezzar's armies began hostilities against Edom. He tumbled the cliff dwelling eagles from their nest as predicted with these words:

"All the men of thy confederacy have brought thee on thy way, even to the border; the men that were at peace with thee have deceived thee, and prevailed against thee. Shall I not in that day, saith Jehovah, destroy the wise men out of Edom . . . (Obadiah 7, 8).

The siege did not completely annihilate the Edomites. They made strenuous efforts to rebuild the ruins, but in 312 B.C., the Arabs, known as the Nabataeans, invaded Edom and gradually rose to a position of great wealth and power. Edom ceased to be (Obadiah 10).

And what about Petra? The Nabataeans were conquered by the Roman emperor Trajan in A.D. 106, after which their civilization soon disappeared. Today, Petra is a desolate waste with no human habitation. It is a refuge for wild animals. No matter what many prophetic visionaries assume will happen to Petra, the city will never be restored. God's words never fail to materialize (Ezekiel 35:7-9).

The Chaldean Chronicle

The metropolis of the Babylonian empire was built on both sides of the river, Euphrates, in the form of a square. A deep and broad moat, flooded from the river, protected the city. According to Herodotus, it included an area of about 200 square miles. Probably nine-tenths of this great space consisted of gardens, parks and fields. The city was enclosed within a double row of high walls, the height being about 335 feet. The thickness of the walls was about seventy-five feet, wide enough to have rows of small houses on each side with a space between them large enough for the passage of a chariot. The city had one hundred bronze gates equally spaced on all sides and twenty-five gates sloping to the water's edge. This will be an important factor in the eventual conquest of the city.

During the long reign of Nebuchadnezzar, some forty

years, Babylon flourished. He was even used as a servant of God to punish the nation of Israel for idolatry; but, at his death, the power he had evolved rapidly crumbled. Everything and everyone was corrupted with demonic religion. She thought of herself as being "the shining one," even reaching above the stars of God, but her judgement was inevitable (Jeremiah 51:9).

The fall of Babylon is more than just history. What happened and the reason why have a bearing on this generation in which we are living. It was in the area *religion* that the Chaldean civilization started to disintegrate. In addition to political strife, new religious ideas were causing chaos in the whole world of the time. Nabonidus and later his son Belshazzar, engaged in certain religious acts which the priests did not hesitate to denounce. This will unfold as we continue to see the revealing facets of a remarkable plan which is prevailing even in the twentieth century.

Nearly 200 years in advance, the prophet Isaiah foretold Babylon's doom. Take notice of the key phrases and the wisdom portrayed:

> "Both these things shall come to you suddenly, *in a single day*: Complete bereavement and widowhood shall come upon you—For your many sorceries and the great number of your spells. *Let the astrologers stand forth* to save you . . . " (Isaiah 47:3, 13).

It was ironic that as the prophecy gradually came to view, the famous astrologers were unable to predict the fate of the city nor offer a solution to prevent it. Greater significance was that it fell "in a single day" or the night of Tishri 16, in 539 B.C.

Again, the prophet Isaiah astonishes the reaching mind. He discloses the name of the conqueror:

> "Thus says Yahweh to his anointed, *to Cyrus*, whom he has taken by his right hand to subdue nations before him and strip the loins of kings . . . For your

sake I send an army against Babylon" (Isaiah 45:1; 43:14).

With expectation, in 559 B.C., a prince by the name of Cyrus became king of a southern Persian tribe. About five years later, he made himself ruler of all Persia, with history recognizing him as one of the most sensational conquerors of all time.

How could a city of such magnitude fall in one day? What strategy did the Bible predict? Isaiah further informs us:

> "I myself, Yahweh, made all things, I alone spread out the heavens. When I gave the earth shape, did anyone help me? . . . I am he who says to the ocean: Be dry. *I will dry up your rivers*. I am he who says to Cyrus, my shepherd . . . " (Isaiah 44:24, 27, 28).

The Babylonians were filled with wine, celebration, and noises of religious frenzy. Taking advantage of the situation, Cyrus the Great diverted the waters of the Euphrates River and marched up the riverbed. Isaiah again adds that "the two-leaved doors so that even the gates will not be shut." Whether the gates were left open by accident or a conspiracy, the forces marched in. That very night, Babylon fell.

Babylon did not immediately become a ruin. There were many attempts to rebuild the city. Even Alexander the Great had aspirations of making it the capital of his eastern empire; but after his early death, Babylon slowly fell to decay.

It has been suggested by some modern-day religious seers that Babylon possibly would be restored, using as reference, Babylon the Great, as mentioned in the book of Revelation. However, God's Word supercedes that of human profundity and inference. It is stated emphatically that:

> "She will never be inhabited, nor will she reside for generation after generation. . . . And there the haunters of waterless regions will certainly lie down, and their houses must be filled with eagle

owls . . . and jackals must howl . . . and the big snake will be in the palaces . . . " (Isaiah 13:20-22).

The English archaeologist, Layard, after visiting Babylon in the nineteenth century, reported that "the site of Babylon is a naked and hideous waste." A look at dead history can point to a live future. The best method of proof is to put a prophecy to the test of time and circumstances. With that method, the reader will first be amazed, then convinced of its accuracy. It should provide incentive to study further prophecies dealing with today which will be found equally reliable.

Chapter 3
Israel's Portent

For not everybody who is descended
from Israel really belongs to Israel.

Romans 9:6

In the late nineteenth century, the Romanoffs, beginning with Alexander III, were inclined to support a high degree of uniformity throughout the empire. It was difficult to attain because the development of the Russian frontier had brought millions of alien people under the Czar's rule. The social problems of the underprivileged peasants increased to an incontrollable degree. They were encouraged to believe that the Jews were responsible for all of Russia's troubles. The Jews were defenseless victims of the Russiafication program, for although they numbered over five million, they were scattered throughout Western Russia and possessed no one locality which they could call their own. They eventually were subjected to periodic persecution and massacres. This was the classical diversion and scapegoat stratagem that was to be repeated with effectiveness in the twentieth century by Adolf Hitler.

Hitler, after thirteen years of persistent and artful maneuvering, finally became Chancellor of Germany. It was January 1933, and he immediately set out to achieve his program and the glories of the New Order. This included the destruction of what was probably the most distinquished Jewry in Europe. In a series of schemes and systematic perspectives that extended from 1933 to 1938, Hitler succeeded in destroying German Jewry, which included thousands of *German-Christian Jews*. All that lived were imprisoned in concentration camps with their wealth con-

28

fiscated. After 1943, the news of the holocaust leaked out, and the total number of deaths resulting from mass annihilation was horrifying. In 1946, a census of the Jewish population was taken throughout Europe. Prior to the war, there were nearly 9,000,000 Jews reported. The census indicated only about 3,000,000 survived—nearly 6,000,000 slaughtered.

Although the Nazi regime of Hitler had been defeated, anti-Semitism is still strong. Constrained by increased persecution of the Jews, the Zionist movement asserted their independence, fought for it, and won it. This was May 14, 1948, and the question of Israel's restoration became eminent on the minds of orthodox Jews and many religionists of Christendom. It was suggested that the regathering to Palestine was in fulfillment of prophecy and an index that Armageddon was related to Middle East confrontations. The Bible proves beyond doubt that the nation of Israel was God's chosen people. However, before considering the significance of the modern day Zionist movement, a projection into the portrait of Ancient Israel would be enlightening as to whether the past is linked with the present.

Carving of Antiquity

An impartial examination of creation reveals the works of a Master Scientist. Man has expanded his knowledge of science and has achieved many marvelous accomplishments in the area of science and technology. However, when it comes to human relations, man has been found sadly deficient (Jeremiah 10:23). In order to understand God more fully, we must first comprehend that he has a far greater scope of time and space, and this is found to be true when he laid a foundation for a Kingdom under a *promised seed*.

The world of righteousness was future and was foreordained by God. In time, he promised the "seed of a woman" who would destroy the serpentlike adversary and those serving his world (Genesis 3:15).

To accomplish his imperious plan, God dealt exclusively with the nation of Israel as his people *for a time.* The choosing of one nation in lieu of another did not result in partial treatment (Deuteronomy 10:17). By reason of the ransom sacrifice of Christ Jesus, "all sorts of men" would be saved. Remember, more was expected of the chosen, requiring them to make an account for serious wrongdoings against the law. The nations roundabout were permitted to continue their life course without interference and still benefit from God's generous provisions (Matthew 5:45). He selected one nation as a *living example* of his principles and dealings with man. He selected that nation because of his love for Abraham, but while dealing independently with Israel, he was working out a purpose to bless all nations later. Through them, he revealed himself and his loving attributes, especially that of long-suffering, when he chastised Israel many times. His wisdom was also manifested in the way of preserving the truth through one nation and holding it together under a Law covenant, *as long as the covenant was in force.* This is vitally important when considering the political implications of Jerusalem today.

The apostle Paul had shown that the dealings God had with the ancient state of Israel were to be a "shadow of the things to come." The new state was established over thirty-four hundred years ago according to divine justice. In Canaan, God entered into a covenant with Abraham to give the land to his seed and from the continuation of this seed, a blessing to all the nations of the earth. The covenant was ratified when both Abraham and God established the necessary sacrificial basis to bind the covenant legally. This would, in time, establish *"the city having real foundations and the builder and creator of which is God"* (Hebrews 11:10).

After some 430 years in Egypt under the dominating hand of Pharaoh, Abraham's descendants were allowed to leave under the direction of Moses who was commissioned by God to become their mediator. According to the patriarchal law, a near relative could reclaim or repurchase relatives that had become slaves. God, therefore, had become the rightful repurchaser of Israel.

The population of the nation became so numerous that it was impossible to organize it into a patriarchal society, so it became necessary to form the state of Israel with a *theocratic* or *God-ruling* government. This arrangement was not a new creation. It had its roots in the lives of the patriarchs—the same God that had appeared to Abraham, Isaac and Jacob (Exodus 3:14). Thus it is that the people followed Moses out of bondage and sojourned to Sinai, where God's covenant with the patriarchs received its ratification and was expressed in these words:

"And you shall be unto me a kingdom of priests and a holy nation" (Exodus 19:6).

The Ten Commandments were followed by a series of some 600 additional laws which were transmitted to the people and which finally became the Torah of which the Pentateuch is the written record. Supernaturally, there was a loud trumpet sound at Mt. Sinai to denote that the government, under the Sovereign Power, was now in force.

The law constitution made provisions for a dynasty of Israelite kings to be chosen by God. Importantly, and unlike the rulers of the nations, they were not absolute monarchs. The constitutional kings were kept separate from the dynasty of the high priests. They were only vassal kings in that they sat on God's throne, not their own.

Adaptation to Idolatry

After entering the Promised Land, there were many adjustments that had to be made. The settling down from a nomadic existence to an agricultural life was not easy. In the process of adapting, the nation came under the influence of the sensuous cults of the nations, with their child sacrifices and sacred prostitution. Resistance to these tendencies were offered by the judges, but their influence was only a temporary safeguard. However, the capture of the Ark of the Covenant and the destruction of Shiloh by the Philistines made a deep impression upon the tribes. Samuel took advantage of the situation and brought about a reform which led to the abolition of the Baal worship in Israel.

It wasn't long before Israel was making importunate demands for a king (I Samuel 8:5-7). Saul became their first king; however, he did not realize the hopes placed in him and eventually fell to disobedience and later, to rebellion. He was followed by David, of the tribe of Judah. During his reign of forty years, he succeeded in effecting true unity, cementing it by making Jerusalem both the national capital and the seat of the Ark. This work of centralization was carried on and developed to a greater extent by his son, Solomon, the wisest of all the ancient kings. This wisdom was personified in his 1,005 songs and 3,000 proverbs. His reign became clearly defined by peace and prosperity throughout the kingdom. And yet, with all his accomplishments and the trend to pure worship, Solomon ended up a failure.

Triumph of the Prophets

Rehoboam, a son of Solomon, came to the throne at the age of forty-one and reigned seventeen years. When he was anointed at Shechem, he was met by representatives of ten tribes who demanded relief from the crushing burden of taxation that Solomon had laid upon them. Following the advice of his young courtiers, Rehoboam gave an insolent reply, and the ten tribes revolted. Only Judah and a part of Benjamin remained loyal to him.

The northern kingdom was assigned to Jeroboam; and, as a matter of policy, he revived the ancient calf-worship at Bethel and Dan. The Levites refused to obey him and returned to Judah. He then proceeded to form a new priesthood. For the next forty years, Israel was governed by the house of Omri. Through him, the strong hill of Samaria was chosen as the site of his capital. The princes of his house cultivated an alliance with the kings of Judah, which was consummated by the marriage of Jehoram and Athaliah, but accomplished no notable change. The adoption of Baal-worship led to a reaction in the nation and brought about the triumph of the prophets. Although the kings that followed pursued greatness, it was short-lived with the last king of Jehu's line. The encroaching power of Assyria put an end to the independence of Israel and captured the capital city of Samaria. Some gleanings of the ten tribes yet remained in the land, but even these were eventually gathered up and carried to Assyria as slaves.

The tribe of Judah still possessed the scepter as promised by reason of the everlasting covenant made with David. The kingdom enjoyed greater stability than Israel and lasted for a longer period of time. However, continuous conflicts eventually plagued Judah—not only with the ten-tribe kingdom—but also with the nations surrounding their domain. As in the case of Israel, idolatry was later practiced on a large scale. This brought about a decree from God of complete desolation of Jesusalem and its temple.

God's long-suffering with his disobedient people is highlighted through the service of the prophets. They repeatedly reminded both the northern and southern kingdoms of the covenant made with their forefathers and the consequences that would result if they would continue to follow their fatal course. They would not heed the warnings and many times sought to kill the prophets. They were criticizing the justice of God who had brought upon them suffering for sins their ancestors had committed. Jeremiah renounced this popular notion and sought to impress upon the people that each was responsible for his own sin and bore the misfortunes that were to overtake them. Ezekiel emphasized that, in reality, the personal relationship with God meant the city, the temple and pure worship.

Nevertheless, the prophets foresaw a restoration of the *Israel of God* which *one day* was to lead all nations to the worship of the one and only God, Jehovah (Jeremiah 16:19). The key to this universal reality was to be the *new covenant* (Jeremiah 31:31-34).

State of Termination

During the short reign of Jehoiakim, the Babylonian armies laid siege against Jerusalem. Nebuchadnezzar entered the city and looted the temple utensils of silver and gold. The seige lasted for more than seventeen months. The famine in the city was so severe that the mothers were eating their own babies (Lamentations 2:19, 20). Owing to the revolt of Zedekiah, Nebuchadnezzar and the Chaldean army appeared again before the walls, and after a siege which was prolonged to a period of one year, five months, and seven days, the palace was captured, and the temple itself was entirely destroyed. For a period of seventy years, according to Jeremiah's prophecy, the city lay in ruins until Cyrus, in 539 B.C., gave permission for its rebuilding and likewise the rebuilding of the temple (Jeremiah 50:4, 5).

It was related by God's Word that 42,360 Jews left Babylon, along with 7,337 men and women slaves, and 200 male and female singers (Ezra 2:1-67). It was a four month journey to the land of Judah. Weeping from joy would stain their faces as they once again relied upon God's guidance and provisions to return. They would again acknowledge and renew the covenant of their forefathers.

A vital fact now comes into play, one that should influence our decision on the Zionist movement today. The purpose of Israel returning *would have no political inference*. Their objective *would not have been to re-establish a kingdom* because they were subjugated to Persian domination. Therefore, their primary purpose for enduring such a difficult journey *was to restore pure worship* by rebuilding the temple in Jerusalem (Ezra 1:1-4). Israel did not return to its earlier predominancy as an independent nation; however, it did become a Hebrew commonwealth.

The long interval between the time of Nehemiah and that of Pompey [nearly four centuries] was full of sad events for Jerusalem. In 320 B.C., Alexander the Great visited the city and entered the temple. During the years following that date, the city was many times taken and retaken, pillaged, its temple robbed, its inhabitants slain by the thousands in the wars between the kings of Syria and those of Egypt. The worst form of desecration took place under Antiochus Epiphanes who established a gymnasium in which heathen sports were taught to the Hebrew youth in order to turn them away from their natural faith. He even set up an idol on the holy altar and caused offerings to be rendered to a pagan deity. The period of independence, which was enjoyed under the Maccabees, witnessed the expiring glories of Jerusalem as the capital of the strictly Jewish nation.

Herod the Great, as king of Judea, became master of the city in 37 B.C. He began building the temple in Jerusalem about 21 B.C., after it was destroyed the second time. The Jews would not recognize it as a third temple [only the rebuilding of Zerubbabel's temple]. By the time Jesus, the Son of God was born, about October 2, B.C., drastic changes had already taken place in the form of Judaism. Of both the Jews in Palestine and those dispersed to almost every part of the civilized world, it became evident that they had begun to absorb the ideas of the various sects of Hellenism. Previously, their assembly halls were known as the Beth ha'Keneset [house of prayer] and later, under the influence of the Greeks, came to be called *synagogues*.

Eventually, Judaism began to divide into sects which served as pressure groups, both religiously and politically. They were present during the ministry of Christ as well as the apostles. They were the:

Essenes, a body of devout religious persons or Hellenistic Puritans. They were strictly disciplined and believed in the doctrine of pronounced dualism of the body and soul—the body being mortal and the soul, possessing immortality.

Sadducees, a party of the rich, called the "proud Jews." They were materialistic and did not share in the Messianic hope or the possibility of a resurrection.

Scribes that formed a sect and were preciously associated with the "pious ones" [Hasidim]. They were lawyers, so to speak, of the Law of Moses.

Pharisees, known as habherim [neighbors] and were quite influential with the populus. They believed the soul to be immortal and that only the souls of good men would pass into another body, with the wicked into eternal torment.

Herodians, another pressure group which followed Herod and supported his objections.

Sanhedrin Court, a combination of priests and leaders from the aforementioned sects. They were influential even as far as Rome.

These pressure groups were brought forth by Satan in an effort to decompose the integrity of the Son of God, but the great truth that he revealed exposed their intention, and likewise, will benefit us with reference to the authoritativeness of the Zionist movement of today.

Condemnatory Assertions

The Abrahamic covenant had its fulfillment in the "seed that would bring blessings to all the nations of the earth." The Law covenant, given to Moses some 430 years later, was an addition to the one given Abraham. It served to protect the Israelites from the unsavory influence of the idolatrous nations surrounding them. More importantly, it should have led them to Christ, as a tutor, to create the need for a ransomer and at the same time, a permanent sacrifice.

It was impossible for the Jews to keep the Law perfectly due to their imperfection. Why then, are we to view the Law as being perfect? Because it perfectly served the purpose of the Creator to the letter. After it was fulfilled in Christ, *it was brought to a legal end* and along with it, *the ancient state of Israel.*

When speaking of the "conclusion of the Law," it should remind us of Paul's words to the Colossian congregation:

> "Having cancelled the written code, with its regulations, that was against us and that stood opposed to us; he took it away, nailing it to a tree" (Colossians 2:14).

Naturally, this was symbolically stated. According to the customs of Asia at the time of Christ, debts or outmoded laws were cancelled by nailing them to a tree in public view. Jesus was born under that law mediated by Moses; however, when he was baptized in A.D. 29, and anointed with God's Spirit, he became the Mediator of a new covenant. *The new covenant was not made with fleshly Israel,* but spiritual Israel [to be discussed later] (Galatians 3:29).

Contractual Release

A startling revelation pertaining to the end of the Jewish nation can be found in the controversial parable of the "Rich Man and Lazarus." A reminder is necessary as we refer to the sixteenth chapter of Luke, that doctrine is not being considered. Only Jesus' reflections of the "conclusion of an ai•on" [age].

This parable or illustration was spoken from Perea, probably early in the year of A.D. 33. In order to fully understand the chapter and the inference of Jesus' words, consider the context and how it affects the meaning. Among the observers were the Pharisees. Their wind-blown garbs of nobility only enhanced the unyielding look of suspicion as Jesus related his treatise.

Jesus identified the rich man as the Pharisees who looked down on others, especially those having the reputation of being sinners (Luke 16:14). Therefore, the beggar would represent those who repented and became followers of Jesus Christ. They desired the spiritual food that promotes maturity, but only received crumbs, as it were. Their death symbolically represents a complete change as to their standing before God (Colossians 2:13). As for the unrepentant Pharisees and prominent leaders from other religious affiliations, they were dead to their former position as God's chosen people *and were buried*. The change for Lazarus came on the day of Pentecost, the time when the new covenant replaced the old Law covenant. They symbolically came to be in Abraham's bosom, i.e., *God's favor*, and became a distinct part of spiritual Israel. "Bosom position" refers to a custom of one reclining in front of another for a meal. The guest reclines on the left arm with the right free. Therefore, one's head would be in the bosom position of the other. It was to occupy a special position of favor to the one nearest the king (Compare John 1:18; 13:23, 25; 21:20).

The rich man's torment was the realization that they have been rejected as God's chosen nation (Acts 7:54). In view of this conclusion, the "fixed chasm" would signify the uncompromising nature between the ancient state of Israel and spiritual Israel.

The *key* to understanding the parable and the actuality that the ancient state of Israel had to be disused on a legality is the unrelated statement in verse eighteen.

"Anyone who divorces his wife and marries another woman commits adultery, and the man who marries a divorced woman commits adultery."

The covenant relationship that existed between the nation

38

of Israel and God was as a *husband and wife* (Jeremiah 3:14). However, when Jesus made his appearance, the opportunity was extended to the Jews to become part of his bride under the new covenant (John 3:28-30). Accordingly, there had to be a release from the Law, i.e., a release from their marriage to God. If not, they would come to be in an adulterous relationship. It is what led to the complete change in the conditions of the "rich man and Lazarus" (Romans 7:4). This would eliminate the possibility of a future restoration of the fleshly nation of Israel.

Abstract Expressions

Romans 11:26 makes a straightforward statement, "All Israel will be saved." The evidence is obvious that the term, "all Israel," embraces spiritual Israel. The same Scripture ascribes the "full number of Gentiles" as being a part of Israel, and Galatians 3:28 confirms this realization. The majority of Israel forfeited the privilege, thus paving the way for the nations. "For not all who are descended from Israel are Israel."

Jesus further warns ancient Israel that "The Kingdom of God *will be taken from you* and be given to a nation producing its fruits" (Matthew 21:43). The nation then and today failed to produce Kingdom fruits deserving of repentance. When speaking before Pontius Pilate and clamoring for the death of Jesus, the Israelite leaders said:

"Anyone who claims to be a king opposes Caesar. . . . We have no king but Caesar" (John 19:12, 15).

The Kingdom is only given to the nation that accepts the Kingdom of God. It is the nation that accepts God's Anointed One. Since it is God's Spirit that builds such a nation, *it is no political nation* nor is it a nation *that claims its own sovereignty.*

Emphasizing the requisite of producing fruit and the

possible repudiation of fleshly Israel if they fall short, John the Baptizer warned the leaders:

> "And do not think you can say to yourselves, we have Abraham as our father . . . The ax is already at the root of the trees . . . " (Matthew 3:9, 10).

Paul uses the illustration of a cultivated olive tree to explain the mystery or sacred secret of what constitutes spiritual Israel. The "root is holy" so it would have reference to the source of all life, Yahweh. It further discloses that " . . . some of the branches have been broken off, and you, though a wild olive shoot [gentile], have been grafted in among the others and now share in the nourishing sap from the olive root" (Romans 11:16, 17). The parable of the Wedding Banquet reiterates the invitation extended to the Israelites as a nation, to become a kingdom of priests, but they paid no attention and went off—one to his field, another to his business. The king then ordered his servants to go to the street corners and invite anyone they could find. The king was enraged and sent his army to *destroy the murderers and burn their city* (Matthew 22:1-7). With this thought before us, consideration will be given to the final and most substantial manifestation of the condemnatory assertion.

The Final Tally

The final marked change in the political history of Jerusalem was its conquest by Titus in A.D. 70. It was upon the buildings of the temple that the disciples looked with wonderment as Jesus prophesied that "by no means will a stone be left here upon a stone and not be thrown down" (Matthew 24:1, 2). This complete destruction was foretold in the year A.D. 33.

The prophecy extended its predictions, for the sake of accuracy, with further insinuations that "your enemies will build around you a fortification with pointed stakes and will encircle you and distress you from every side" (Luke

19:43). It was also prophesied that pangs of distress would precede The Final Tally. They were to be part of a composite sign in answer to the disciples' question expounded to Jesus. It is also significant as to the meaning of what is taking place today.

"And so he was sitting upon the Mount of Olives. The disciples came to him privately saying—Tell us, when these things shall be—And what the sign of thy presence and the conclusion of the age?" (Matthew 24:3).

In A.D. 41, Claudius was crowned, succeeding the assassination of King Galigula. He installed Agrippa over all the districts, and once more the Jews had their own king one who followed the Pharisees and was a strict Jew. Claudius died in A.D. 44, and the rule of the procurators was restored. The Jews were eventually provoked into a melee and a massacre took place in the temple and bloodshed occurred between the Samaritans and Galileans.

The country became filled with robbers, and the High Priest was murdered in the temple. False prophets appeared and there was one struggle after another, even Jewish forces against each other. During this time, the city of Jerusalem was hard pressed by famine and without financial means to purchase what was needed. Finally in A.D. 66, according to Jesus' words, the conflict began.

There was a series of uprisings in various cities in which the Roman garrisons were massacred by Jewish rebels. Cestius Gallus marched his armies on Jerusalem and laid siege to the city, but for some unaccountable reason, he lifted the siege suddenly and retreated. The Jews were convinced that divine favor was on their side and reorganized their forces for battle.

The Roman armies under General Titus fulfilled Jesus' words by marching for the final siege. A wall was constructed around the city some 4½ miles long, being completed in only three days. It was made of pointed stakes,

41

angled in toward the walls of the city. The results—Jerusalem fell in August with the walls breached and the gates burned. *The Jewish System of Things ended with the destruction of the temple.* Those not massacred were sold into slavery, with the exception of a handful that fled to the remaining fortress of Masada. Among the many indiscriminate prophetic and historic applications made by Hal Lindsey in his book, *The 1980's—Countdown to Armageddon,* the one dealing with the Masada is no different. I am flabbergasted that he would consider the "Masada Connection" as being heroic. Jesus foretold the destruction of all inhabitants of Jerusalem who did not flee to the mountainous regions. Rather than the 950 Jews being martyrs, we should consider them among those who rejected the Son of God as their Messiah. In addition, they committed suicide, a practice condemned by the Law of Moses as well as principles recorded in God's Word for Christians.

The fact that God had ceased to be with the nation of Israel and was with the apostles and disciples of Jesus [as demonstrated at Pentecost] gives strong substantial proof that it was the end of the state of Israel. After speaking of the fulfillment of Joel's prophecy, Peter additionally said to the inquiring Jews, "Let all the house of Israel therefore know assuredly that God has made him both Lord and Christ, this Jesus whom you crucified" (Acts 2:36).

The Jewish law teacher, Gamaliel, gave the final tally. When the apostles were brought before the council, the high priest and others were enraged and wanted to kill them. Gamaliel's words were emphatic:

> "Men of Israel, take care what you do with these men . . . for if this plan or this undertaking is of men, it will fail; but if it is of God, you will not be able to overthrow them . . . " (Acts 5:34-39).

The works of the apostles did prove to be "of God," but that which was overthrown proved to be the end of an age.

Zion or Zionism?

The purpose of Zionism was to open up a national Jewish state or homeland for all Jews. In 1896, the Viennese journalist and playwright Theodore Herzl proposed a self-governing community and made an extensive effort to revitalize the spirit of the progressive Jewish thinkers. The World Zionist Organization was formed with Herzl as president; however, the movement leaders were nationalists and not devout religionists. So the motive was to have his people socially equalized with the rest of the world and politically free. Although Palestine was the preferable location, he would have settled for British East Africa.

Jewish youth groups, who called themselves Hoveve-Zion, started what was called "practical Zionism." They insisted that only Palestine was acceptable for establishing their homeland. Herzl foresaw a problem in the lack of influence of such a new government, especially when confronting the Ottoman Empire who had claim to the land of Israel. He therefore decided to put faith in the British Empire.

Britain made the Balfour Declaration in 1917. It promised to promote the establishment of a national homeland for the Jewish people in Palestine. Under the mandate, many from economically poor and wealthy backgrounds came to Palestine. A large city was built at Tel-Aviv. Hitler and World War II brought about many problems, but the one that has continued to this day is the influx of the Jewish people which suppressed the Arab states, the citizens of which considered Palestine their homeland. British troops were forced to decline the entrance of shiploads of Jewish immigrants to the area. Finally, with negligible results, the British government withdrew their forces and the Republic of Israel was proclaimed and recognized by the United Nations. Ever since that time, Zionism has been far from the peaceful conditions that were expected. There have been continuous struggles with her Arab neighbors as well as internal strife. This was due to racial and irrational disagreements. There are many Jews who strongly oppose Zionism, indicating that Judaism is not one of race, nationality or politics, but one of religion.

The increased prominence of Israel in world affairs led many overweening prophesiers to fit each distinct incident to Bible prophecy. It not only misinformed the populus of the signs of the times, but falsely elevated individuals to a status of divine appointment. The foregoing medium of Biblical proof should convince the inquirer that the state of Israel ended with the destruction of the temple in A.D. 70. Those who are Jews inwardly and circumcised of the heart live in the realities and not on the "shadows" of the past (Romans 2:28, 29). Critical questions arise as to whether there must be a rebirth of the Republic of Israel for Bible prophecy to be fulfilled. Consider the following determinative summary: *To this day, has the new republic trusted in God for protection against their enemies?*

In 1908, the rise of nationalistic Turks refused to consider a surrender of their rights to Palestine in the form of a Zionist document. On December 9, 1917, the Jews were delivered from the Turks and eventually, the mandate for Israel's rights were legally assigned to Great Britain by the League of Nations. On March 29, 1946, the Anglo-American committee recommended certain steps to be taken for the establishment of Palestine. This was transformed into a trusteeship of the United Nations. On May 14, 1948, David Ben-Gurion, first premier of the new state, proclaimed the State of Israel with its temporary capital at Tel Aviv.

The modern Republic of Israel had not heeded the warnings of their forefathers. They disregarded the council of God and became a friend of the world, seeking their assurance of existence and recognition (Isaiah 31:1). To ward off their attackers to this day, they have used devastating armaments secured from antitypical "Egypt." There is no tangible reason to think that Israel has God's backing. *To this day, do the Jews have a temple on Mount Moriah, consecrated to God?*

In the strength of the Most High, the Israelite remnant left Babylon and made an arduous journey to their desolate homeland. The purpose was to reoccupy the land and put spiritual interest first by rebuilding Jerusalem and erecting a temple. When they adhered to the prophets' words, they prospered. Their property was not confiscated by intruders, nor did they suffer economically. They did not bring up children to fall to war or delinquency (Isaiah 65:21-24). This is not true of the modern day restoration of Israel.

They immigrated into the land not lying desolate. The temple site was occupied by the Mohammedan mosque of Omar. Rather than the dry bones of Ezekiel being recreated and reanimated by the outpouring of the Spirit of God, the Jews settled in Palestine with a "military force" to establish the Republic. There is no recognizable difference in the Jews of today than previously. When restored to their homeland, those Jewish prisoners did not fall into the bondage of idolatry, yet they came into a greater and more dangerous bondage, that of the religious system of Judaism—the system dominated by the precepts and traditions of men. *To this day, does the new state have a priesthood of the chosen family of Aaron?*

The ancient state of Israel had an official priesthood vested in the paternal house of Aaron, the High Priesthood limited to the family line. He wore a breastpiece that contained the Urmin and Thummin. It enabled him to determine important decisions on state problems. On Atonement Day, the High Priest carried the blood of the sacrificial bull and goat into the Most Holy and spattered it seven times in front of the Ark. It pictured Jesus Christ as entering heaven itself, in God's presence, to present the atoning value for all mankind.

If the presence of the Messiah was not accepted by the new Republic of Israel, the priesthood should have, likewise, been restored. One problem, however, is that there is no circumcised Jew that could produce valid credentials proving that he was the real descendant of Aaron or the Levites because all the records were destroyed in 70 A.D. Also, take in consideration that the percentage of intermarriage with non-Jews is phenomenal. In fact, it was so critical that the issue was presented to the Israeli Supreme Court for a decision. *The New York Times* of February 2, 1970, featured an article entitled, "Split on Defining—Jew—Grows in Israel."

The Ark of the Covenant pictures the presence of God (Exodus 25:22). Since the Ark was never located after the destruction of 607 B.C., and was not in view when the temple curtain was separated during the death of Jesus, it indicates that his presence has not been felt by the Israelites as a nation since that time. The Christian Greek Scriptures make it clear that the release from sin and death is by the paying of a price (I Corinthians 6:20; 7:23). It originally was offered to the nation of Israel. It is now available to all. *To this day, is the Republic bringing forth fruits of the Kingdom?*

The Kingdom is open to any person who maintains moral and spiritual innocence (Galatians 5:19-21). However, besides combating fleshly tendencies to maintain this purity, those who gain entrance into the Kingdom must bear the fruit of the Kingdom. The bearing of fruit refers to making expressions about the Kingdom and demonstrating them in our lives. The Republic of Israel has imitated the world with "works of the flesh" overflowing in the ranks of their citizenship.

As a Republic representing a political entity rather than a theocratic nation, the modern state finds itself entangled in the power struggles of today. Strong religious controversies separate Jew and Arab, but the fuse igniting their wars are issues not related to the Bible. They fail to effect Micah's prophecy of restoration when he declared that "they will beat their swords into plowshares and their spears into pruning shears . . . they will learn war no more."

Another factor of prophetic indifference is the issue of abortion. Israel's Knesset [Parliament] passed a law to legalize abortion. It permits abortion for women under 16 or over 40 if the pregnancy resulted from illicit sexual activity. In effect, it gave legality to a common practice in Israel. One study disclosed that nearly 50 percent of Israeli women have had at least one abortion by the age of 40.

The same problems plague the Republic of Israel that afflict the rest of the world. Pollution threatens the principal reservoir systems, especially with the increasing amount of sewage and nitrate fertilizers being poured into the Jordan River.

Internal factions are also prevalent. The Orthodox Jews of Bnei Braq, Israel, wanted to close their town's main avenue to auto traffic on the Sabbath. As a result, many engaged in violent clashes with the police and secular Jews. *The New York Times* had reported that "five policemen were injured, two seriously, by rocks and bottles."

It seems to the world that the differences between the Arabs and Israelis appear great; however, the Jerusalem criminologist, Menahen Amir, asserts that Jews and Arabs in the underworld are using this fact to exploit drug sales. Five Jews and Arabs were charged together with smuggling hugh quantities of hashish from Jordan. It was also reported that Israel has had a 35-percent overall increase in crime in the last five years; burglaries are up 200-percent. Dr. Amir further states that many engaging in robbery, prostitution and gambling are religious Jews. As in the first century, people make God's word invalid while holding to man-made religious traditions. God's Son said that such worship is in vain. *To this day, are they eating and drinking and rejoicing under God's king of the line of David?*

The destruction of the kingdoms of Israel and Judah were according to God's exercise of kingly power and justice. The modern Jerusalem built by the Jews to the west of the ancient walled city has no Messianic king of David's family reigning in it. It is, rather, the capital city of the Republic of Israel.

Since the days of Jesus Christ, the earthly city of Jerusalem is not what counts. Rather, the thing that counts is what the Jewish city symbolized at the time it was destroyed in 607 B.C. It symbolized God's Kingdom by means of his Anointed One, and it is that kingdom that is trampled down by the gentiles. Since Jesus Christ was raised in the Spirit, he now "dwells in unapproachable light whom not one of men has seen or can see" (I Timothy 6:15, 16). The Prince of Peace is on his heavenly throne, and he will enforce "peace on earth."

In his book, *The Late Great Planet Earth*, Mr. Lindsey says that "What has happened and what is happening right now to Israel is significant in the entire prophetic picture." He further states that "Israel is the fuse of Armageddon."

From the foregoing factual synopsis, the establishment of the Republic of Israel is not the key to the prophetic future. Rather, it should be the reconstruction of Jerusalem and its temple. Until the temple is raised to its previous glory *by God*, all such predictions become as "a sounding piece of brass or a clashing cymbal" that deafens the faculties of the human mind to the realization of the truth.

Heavenly Jerusalem

What is the Jerusalem that is referred to here? From the previous expose, it certainly isn't connected with the modern-day city with many religious and political indifferences. However, according to the Bible, it is a cause for exultation. Paul explains it explicity to the Hebrews:

> "But you have come to Mount Zion and to the city of the living God, the *heavenly Jerusalem*, and to innumerable angels in festal gathering" (Hebrews 12:22).

The Kingdom of God means a government in heaven with a heavenly king, Christ Jesus. This is substantiated by Isaiah when referring to the Son of God and saying, " . . . and the government shall be upon his shoulders."

Where there is a government, there are subjects of that entity who must conform to its requirements. For example, the United States has three branches of government: executive, legislative and judicial. In the legislative branch, the Senate has 100 members while the House of Representatives consists of 435 members. The constitution determines the number that will occupy these seats. The majority of its citizens are not members of the political jurisdiction, but rather subjugated to its power.

God's Kingdom government is similar in many ways. He purposes to bless all humankind with a righteous government that will unite all peoples on earth. That's why we are induced to pray for it when we say, "Thy kingdom come. Thy will be done on earth as it is in heaven." What is shocking to most people on earth is the fact that the membership of the spiritual Israel is limited. The Bible says of them that "they shall be priests of God and of Christ and shall reign with him for a thousand years" (Revelation 20:6).

Today, the terminology, "the body of Christ," is used as indiscriminately as the designation, "Christian." If it were true that all persons claiming to be Christian were of the body of Christ, there would be no subjects to rule over. How shortsighted are this world's religious leaders to believe that God is as disorganized as they are. However, pointing to this very time we are living in, this important issue will be settled. God's Word points to its fulfillment when it says:

"In the days of those kings the God of heaven will set up a Kingdom that will never be brought to ruin. And the Kingdom itself will not be passed on to any other people. It will crush and put an end to all kingdoms, and it will stand forever" (Daniel 2:44).

The birth of this nation took place at Jerusalem in the year 33 A.D., the day called in the Hebrew tongue, "Shabuoth," and "Pentecost" from the Greek. As in the United States government, it is limited to a designated number determined by its Chief Executive Yahweh. It was originally to be made up of the natural Israelites, but due to their rejecting the king to be, the number was to be completed by using people of the nations [gentiles]. The majority of those conforming to his principles and regulations are the subjects of the Kingdom government and will reside, not in heaven, but as Isaiah says:

> "For thus saith Jehovah that created the heavens, the God that formed the earth and made it, that established it and created it not a waste, that formed it to be inhabited" (Isaiah 45:18).

Nowhere in the Scriptures does it indicate that God changed his mind from the original purpose he had of filling the earth with a righteous people who will live forever upon it. He further confirms this by saying that the heavens are my throne and the earth is my footstool.

Solomon, after completing and dedicating the magnificent temple to the Most High said, "But will God truly dwell upon the earth? Look! The heavens themselves cannot contain you; how much less, this house. . . . " If it was impossible then, it certainly is impossible of Jerusalem today.

Chapter 4
Seven Heads of Predominance

Understand, O son of man, that the
vision is for the time of the end.

Daniel 8:17

Great military empires were formed in centuries of civilization, each trying to build more luxurious palaces and to conquer more territory than their predecessors. Each one proved to have no enduring qualities to sustain their rulership beyond what was determined by their own ineptness and a master plan proposed by the Sovereignty of the universe. Because of their determination to dominate mankind with the fear accorded to wild beasts, it was concluded to call this chapter, Seven Heads of Predominance.

The Word of God describes the worldwide political rule over all mankind as a wild beast. Rather than referring to a world power, the terminology is designating a political system that dominates the entire world of its time. Also noticeable is the assertion that these world dynasties were involved with God's people in one form or another from approximately 1750 B.C., when Joseph was sold to an official of Pharaoh's court, to the present Kings of Vexation.

Daniel vividly describes the march of these powers, and it intervolves with the book of Revelation where the apostle John reports a vision in which he saw a wild beast. The thirteenth chapter opens with symbolic rhetoric:

> "And I saw a beast coming out of the sea. He had
> ten horns and seven heads, with ten crowns on his
> horns, and each head a blasphemous name. The
> beast I saw resembled a leopard, but had feet like a
> bear and a mouth like a lion. The dragon gave the

beast his power and his throne and great authority" (Revelation 13:1, 2).

To fully understand the impact of a prophecy upon civilization, it is imperative that the use of symbolic language be
applied accurately. If one envisions that every expression is
surmised to be literal, interpretations will be perplexed,
contradictory and a certain sign that God's Spirit has not
intervened with that one's train of thought.

The Bible is a book of both prophecy and history,
Whenever the Scriptures denote numbers, specific colors,
wild and domestic beasts or verbalism associated with the
earth and sea, the context usually reveals whether it should
be viewed in the literal or symbolic sense.

Throughout history, the populus have discerned this
wild beast in operation and have felt the oppressive power
it yields. Before now, it has been difficult to identify. However, Daniel's words inspire our sense of reason when he
explains that the words were sealed up "until the time of
the end. Many will rove about and the true knowledge will

become abundant" (Daniel 12:4, 10). He further assures the inquirer that only "ones having insight will understand."

The "wild beast" pictures governmental world empires that rule on a global scale. *It is not a federation of all nations,* as many feel, with a central capital. The Scriptures picture it as "coming out of the sea" or out of the sea of mankind (Isaiah 57:20). The agitated masses are estranged from God and continuously stir up seaweed and mire. "Seven" frequently denotes heavenly completeness as in seven creative days, the seven-day week, the seven-year Sabbath and the forty-nine-year Sabbath, a multiple of seven. So "seven heads" mean *seven world powers* that would consecutively march through nearly 5,000 years of man's attempt to rule himself.

The horns depict power, whereas the crowns signify headship or authority. The number "ten" indicates completeness or entirety and pertains to the earth, as in the ten plagues upon Egypt. Therefore, it means the complete number of kings that would prevail over the seven world powers. The beasts that are mentioned in the Scriptures do not literally signify the Russian bear, the American eagle, the lion of Luserne or John Bull of Great Britain, etc. This type of transition is practiced by those who thrive on their ability to exploit the Scriptures for their own purposes. The beasts in Revelation harmonizes with Daniel's prognosis and simply project the various forms of government at different times and places. Since the third world power was in existence at the time of Daniel, it will be necessary to retrogress prior to his captivity.

Powers of Satanic Authority

The valley of the Tigris and the Euphrates Rivers was known as the plain of Shinar. The lower part of it was often called Babylonia—the middle part, Mesopotamia. This is the setting of the early culture recognized as the Babylonians. The founder of this civilization was Nimrod, the Cushite of the Hamitic race of people.

Religion was regarded as polytheistic and the gods merely as supermen. The gods were believed to share the passions and habits of life with the people. Sacrifices were given, not in order to insure for oneself a better future in the life beyond the grave, but only to derive advantages for this life. Many of the magicians and diviners thought they could foretell the future by studying the liver of a sheep slain in sacrifice.

The most important buildings of the Babylonians were the temple towers. Every town had such an edifice, dedicated to its patron deity. The typical towers consisted of several stories, each stepped back and smaller than its predecessor. Each level was given a different symbolic color. One might be black to represent the underworld, another red to indicate this world, and a third blue to symbolize the sky and heavens. The most familiar ziggurat, as they were called, is the *Tower of Babel*. Tradition identifies it with the "Temple of the Seven Lights of the Earth" located in Nebo.

Although Nimrod was king of the first world empire, God would not allow it to become the first world power of the symbolic beast of Revelation. After the civilization was greatly dispersed by God, the remaining inhabitants built towns along the river banks. They made continuous efforts to reunite into a political entity, but the land eventually was captured by a Semitic people who constructed a new state called Assur, from which the name, "Assyria" is derived. Consideration given to Old Babylonia is not unwarranted. It was the start of what became a world empire of false religion, and will become so manifested in future chapters.

Early Disclosures

The glory and splendor of ancient Egypt became the first world power of history. The remains and records tell a story of achievement at which people have never ceased to marvel. Men have often called Egypt the "Cradle of Civilization." The common Biblical name of the country is Misraim.

Herodotus said that it was easier to find a god than a man in Egypt; it may be added that their religion in its later forms deified a multitude of animals, from the bull down to the snake. The two greater myths that stand out is that of Ra, the sun-god, and his family, and that of Osiris and his family. The Egyptian religion was not altogether so polytheistic as it seems, for the same god often had different names in different places. They also had a sublime faith in immortality. The embalming of the body was the result of their faith in the hereafter.

The king was supreme, and he was viewed as the visible god of his subjects—but he was also a man, so he worshipped himself. The nation is prominently mentioned in the Bible because of their efforts to destroy the offspring of Abraham. If this were accomplished, the promised Seed that would bless all the families of the earth would become nonexistent. So God demonstrated his power and humiliated the Egyptians by delivering the nation of Israel from their oppressed captivity. The great struggle with Assyria and the increasing cost of keeping up the temples sapped the strength out of the country. Large armies marched down the Syrian coast and attacked the outposts of the empire. The pharaohs fought them off, but were gradually forced to yield all their territories outside of Egypt. The curtain fell on the first head of the wild beast; although in centuries to follow, they would prove to be a hindrance to the oncoming powers.

The rise of Assyria as the second world power demonstrated the development of militarism in the true sense. Militarism was necessary because during the entire course of Assyrian history, the Assyrians continuously struggled against invasions from mountain tribes who lived just beyond the northern frontier. However, the knowledge of their sadistic tortures gave them an advantage over other militant nations. It struck terror in the hearts of the people. They would lead captives by attaching ropes to hooks that pierced the lips or nose. Prisoners were even skinned alive or impaled atop pointed stakes that entered into the abdomen from the victim's weight.

While at the height of their power, the Babylonians and their reassembled armies seem to have conquered the Assyrians. However, this domination was short-lived. Under the leadership of King Tiglath Pileser I, Babylonia was brought under control. Quite likely, this was possible because of the Assyrian use of horses and chariots. It gave them a decided advantage over their neighbors. Very wisely, they kept their capital in Assyria instead of moving it to Babylon.

The Assyrians were equally able in political administration. They organized their conquered territories into provinces and placed Assyrian governors over them. To help keep down revolts, they adapted the plan of moving the higher classes of the people of a conquered territory to another region and replacing them with other subjects. An excellent example of this was the carrying away of the inhabitants of the northern kingdom of Israel. According to the Assyrian report, forty-two thousand persons were removed from Samaria, the capital city, and scattered throughout Assyria.

While Ashurbanipal was busying himself with domestic matters, trouble was brewing in the northeast. The nomadic Medes poured out of the mountains and overran much of the empire. Babylon again regained her independence and made an alliance with the Medes for a joint attack upon her ancient rival. In a final effort, the Assyrian king allied himself with the restored Egyptian kingdom, but in vain. For three years, the armies of Babylon and the Medes besieged Nineveh. With its fall in 632 B.C., the second head of the wild beast passed into history.

Sequential Dreams

When the Babylonians finally rid themselves of Assyrian overlordship, they organized a "New Babylonia," the so-called Chaldean Empire. Nebuchadnezzar shared in setting up this Neo-Babylonian world power. However, it was only after he would overturn and lay desolate the kingdom of Israel, with its capital in Jerusalem, that he would become the third head of world domination.

The Babylonians re-established the ancient law, literature and art forms, the essentials of the Old Babylonian mode of government, and the economic system of their ancestors with its authority over industry and trade. Marduk returned to his traditional place at the head of the pantheon, but the new order developed into an astral religion. The gods were denuded of their limited human qualities and exalted into transcendent, omnipotent beings. They were actually identified with the planets. Marduk became Jupiter, Ishtar became Venus, and so on.

Two significant results flowed from these conceptions. First, they developed the attitude of fatalism. The gods were elevated beyond mere mortal man, so he had to resign himself to his own fate. It was impossible to absolutely depend upon the gods, so, for the first time in history, there arose the conception of piety among the kings and priests. This concept will be identifiable in later chapters in modern day religions.

Secondly, a stronger spiritual consciousness was generated, and prayers along with hymns were ascribed to Nebuchadnezzar and other leaders, both spiritual and political. In most of them, the gods are addressed as exalted beings who are concerned with justice and righteous conduct on the part of men.

Thirteen years before Jerusalem and its temple were devastated, Nebuchadnezzar came up against the city. King Jehoiakim, King of Judah, failed to take an oath of allegiance to him as overlord. After four years, he was defeated by Nebuchadnezzar and compelled to pay tribute to him.

Three years afterward, he rebelled and was taken prisoner, but was finally permitted to reign as a vassal (2 Kings 24:1). However, according to God's prophecy he became rebellious again and did not surrender to the king. He died in Jerusalem (Jeremiah 22:18, 19).

He was succeeded by his son, Jehoiakim. His reign lasted but three months and ten days, after which time he was taken captive by Nebuchadnezzar and carried to Babylon. After some thirty-seven years, he was released by Evil-merodach who placed him at the head of all captive kings (Jeremiah 52:31-34).

Jehoiakim's uncle, Zedekiah, was made king. Many members of the royal family were taken to Babylon, among them, Daniel and his three companions, Hananiah, Mishael and Azariah. Zedekiah's reign of eleven years was marked by weakness and disorder. He allowed those who had been set free from bondage to be again reduced to slavery, and for this act, the prophet announced the downfall of the nation (Jeremiah 34:8-22). According to God's time table, in 607 B.C., Nebuchadnezzar again besieged Jerusalem by breaking through the walls. He eventually burned the sanctuary and pulverized the city to dust.

This occurrence in history, that happened in 607 B.C., will prove to be a vital factor in future prophecies. World domination, to be exercised by successors to the third head or Babylonian empire, will be exerted in our very lives today. It all began with a dream, sent by God, to Nebuchadnezzar. A dream that he could not recall upon awakening, but so monstrous that it brought terror to his heart. His magicians and professional priests failed to recall the dream. However, after a decree was issued for all wise men to be destroyed, Daniel made himself available and not only gave an interpretation of the dream, but informed the king of the following contents:

"You saw, O king, and behold, a great image. This image, mighty and of exceeding brightness, stood before you, and its appearance was frightening. The head of this image was fine gold, its breast and arms of silver, its belly and thighs of bronze, its legs of iron, its feet partly of iron and clay. As you looked, a stone was cut by no human hand, and it smote the image on its feet of iron and clay, and broke them to pieces" (Daniel 2:31-34).

During the first year of King Belshazzar's reign, Daniel was sent a dream that proved to be more terrifying than Nebuchadnezzar's vision. By entwining the symbolic meanings, a clear-cut understanding can be assured.

Daniel proceeded to interpret the dream saying, "You, O king, you yourself are the head of gold." To be more accurate in the meaning, it denotes the entire dynasty of Babylonian rulers or the third head of the wild beast. Daniel gives additional details in his vision:

> "And four great beasts came up out of the sea, different from one another. The first was like a lion and had eagle's wings. Then as I looked, its wings were plucked and it was made to stand upon two feet like a man" (Daniel 7:3, 4).

It was with a devouring hunger that Babylon wasted the nations surrounding its realm. It had the speed of a lion that was accelerated by two wings (Lamentations 4:19). At the end of Belshazzar's reign, it was predicted by the handwriting on the wall [ME'NE, ME'NE, TE'KEL and PAR'SIN] that Babylon's wings would be plucked, and the nation would be slowed down to a man's pace.

The Medes assisted in the capture of Nineveh and for their share in the overthrow, they received the northern half of the Assyrian Empire. Shortly after, their kinsmen the Persians, under the leadership of Cyrus the Great, overthrew the Medes and founded the Medo-Persian Empire. It was seven years later, or 539 B.C., that Cyrus diverted the course of the Euphrates into another channel and entered the city. Babylon fell as prophesied. A second dream that Daniel received three years after his first one, commenced with this fourth world power of Medo-Persia and will be inserted for consideration.

Nebuchadnezzar's dream now discloses "the breast and arms of silver" symbolizing the Medo-Persian dual power. The phrase "inferior to you" does not refer to the level or quality as compared to Babylon. It was lower than the head of gold and was silver, a metal less precious. Notice as we proceed, the metal becomes less precious as it lowers toward the feet; however, the metal is stronger each time, indicating the increased power they yield. Babylon will always have the distinction of gold by having overturned the kingdom of Jerusalem, and her influence will be evident even in our time. Daniel's two dreams enlighten us further of the fourth head:

> Dan. 7:5 states, "And behold, another beast, a second one, like a bear. It was raised up on one side; it had three ribs in its mouth between its teeth; and it was told, Arise, devour much flesh.'"

> Dan. 8:3, 4 tells us, "I raised my eyes and saw and behold a ram standing on the bank of the river. It

had two horns; and both were high but one was higher than the other, and the higher one came up last. I saw the ram charging westward and north-ward and southward; no beast could stand before him."

In addition to the breast and arms of silver, the dual world power was represented as a "bear" in Daniel's first dream, and in the second, a "ram." The Medes under Darius, after their defeat by his nephew, Cyrus, were in a subservient position, so they could be depicted as one animal. The bear with one side raised and the ram with one horn higher portray the Persian predominance of the powers. The three ribs between the teeth of the bear signify the rams charging directions: westward through Asia Minor and into Thrace; to the north to subdue Babylon and to the south to humble Egypt. The number "three" [to be discussed later], accord-ing to the Scriptures, denotes an emphasizing quality. In this instance, it emphasizes the greed of this fourth head in its quest to conquer.

The Persian Empire was the first great cosmopolitan state. Unlike some of their kinsmen, the Persians appreci-ated culture, and when they came into contact with the higher civilizations of Babylon and Egypt, they borrowed much from them.

At the court of the king, strangers were made welcome. It was this disposition to practice tolerance which so undermined the empire that finally its overthrow became easy. So many foreign peoples visited Persia that they finally outnumbered the native inhabitants. Everywhere there were revolts. The great empire fell in 334 B.C. before a vigorous young conqueror from the west. Daniel's two dreams once again came into play:

> Dan. 7:6 says, "After this I looked, and lo, another like a leopard, with four wings of a bird on its back; and the beast had four heads; and dominion was given to it."

> Dan. 8:5-8 continues, "As I was considering, behold, a he-goat came from the west across the face of the whole earth, without touching the ground; and the goat had a conspicuous horn between his eyes. He came to the ram with the two horns . . . and struck the ram and broke his two horns. . . . Then the he-goat magnified himself

exceedingly; but when he was strong, the great horn was broken, and instead of it there came up four conspicuous horns. . . . "

Alexander the Great, a pupil of Aristotle, was hardly twenty when he came to the throne. He was elected to his father's office as head of the expedition against Persia, and in 334 B.C. began to free Greeks in Asia Minor. On reaching Egypt, Alexander was welcomed by the Egyptians as a deliverer from Persian tyranny. To protect himself from being attacked in the rear by the peoples of northern Africa, he founded the city of Alexander near the mouth of the Nile.

Alexander was no longer king of little Macedon but ruler of the entire known world. Greece, as the belly and thighs of bronze, became the fifth head of the wild beast of Revelation. Her speed of conquest was likened to a leopard, being accelerated by four wings, and viewed as "without touching the ground." The next seven years were spent in conquest of the strange half-civilized people toward the north and east, leaving a line of Greek settlements.

While Alexander was in Babylon planning his conquest of Arabia and the west, he contracted a fever and died before his thirty-third birthday. And according to prophecy, the "one conspicuous horn was broken," and "four came up" in its place.

When Alexander died, the authority passed to his generals, trained tacticians indeed, yet none of them qualified to fill the place of the master. The victors, no longer generals but kings, divided the empire among themselves. Seleucus, the ablest administrator, received Asia from Phrygia to India; western Asia Minor and Thrace fell to Lysimacchus. Ptolemy, who after the death of Alexander, had gone as satrap to Egypt, retained the country as his kingdom, and Cassander, already governor of Macedon, was now recognized as sovereign. According to prophecy, they flaunted their power "toward the four winds of heaven."

Iron-like Authority

We are now approaching the conflict between Greece and Rome, the iron-like power symbolized by the legs of iron in Nebuchadnezzar's dream. One by one, the cities of the Macedonian empire crumbled before the western power. By 30 B.C., General Pompey used his army to defeat the last stronghold of Greece and to gain complete mastery for the Roman world. Greece and Rome came together in a new synthesis which became the Roman World Power, or the sixth head of the wild beast of Revelation. However, amid the era of peace that now confronted Rome, she still ruled with teeth of iron that eventually will become the oppressive spirit against the Son of God. Daniel's reactions are terrifying as he continues:

Dan. 7:7, 8 teaches, "After this I saw in the night

visions, and behold a fourth beast, terrible and dreadful and exceedingly strong; and it had great iron teeth; it was different from all the beasts that went before it; and it had ten horns. I considered the horns, and behold, there came up among them another horn, a little one, before which three of the first horns were plucked up by the roots; and behold, in this horn were eyes like the eyes of a man, and a mouth speaking great things."

Dan. 8:9 again speaks, "Out of one of them came forth a little horn, which grew exceedingly great toward the south, the east, and toward the glorious land."

Rome attested to the fact that they were different and enjoyed a supremacy greater than all civilizations of the preceeding centuries. They were masters of warfare and wise discipline, of moderation and good sense, of sound family life and strong legal instincts. As a reminder, from Rome to the present day kings of vexation, there will be no sharp break in history as before. Its character will change gradually and extend itself into a complete number of other powers, represented by the "ten horns" and into the seventh and last head of the wild beast.

In 11 A.D., Germanicus, nephew of Tiberius Caesar, accompanied his uncle in his campaign on the Rhine. He was consul and appointed to command Gaul and their two armies. Difficulties emerged, and Germanicus was apparently pressed to claim the empire for himself. Shortly after 19 A.D., he died at Antioch, convinced that his wife had poisoned him. Germany came under the influence of Rome until the death of Tiberius.

The changed attitude of the Germanized tribes along the western stretches of the Rhine and the disposition of the legionary garrison presented a danger to Rome. This threat continued until Frankish rule, under the new Germanic empire of Charlemagne, was extended. The expansion of the kingdom and the conversion of the Germans to Catholic Christianity caused the rise of the papacy to a position of unprecedented secular and spiritual authority. The Frankish prince and the Roman pope were convinced that *they were reviving the old Roman Empire in the west.*

In the year 800 A.D., Charles knelt before the altar of Saint Peter's Church as Pope Leo III placed an imperial crown on his head and hailed him emperor amidst the shouts of the people. It then became known as the Holy Roman Empire of Germany, with capitals both east and west. Germany since that time became a dual power with Rome, represented by the sixth head of the wild beast of Revelation. The expanded sixth world power claimed dominion over all Catholic Christendom, except for the British Isles, where they continued to fear and respect the ruling element.

By the second century of the Christian era, the Celtic population of Britain was almost as thoroughly Latinized as the Romans themselves. Early in the fifth century, the Roman legions had been withdrawn from Britain for the defense of Italy and Gaul, leaving the Britons to their own device. During the next two centuries, it was overrun by a

Germanic nation or coalition of nations of Jutes, Angles, and Saxons and laid in Britain the foundations of the English race.

During the sixteenth century, Henry VIII was as nearly an absolute ruler as any English king ever became, and his will was the determining factor in bringing about the break with Rome. England had suffered more than most countries from the financial exaction of the papacy and from the appointment of the pope's favorites to high ecclesiastical offices. The wealthy and corrupt monks and priests were no more popular in England than elsewhere.

Henry needed a male heir to preserve the Tudor line, and there was apparently no hope of such from Catherine. He was eager to marry again and had already chosen Anne Boleyn as his future wife. He, therefore, sought a divorce, or rather an annulment from Pope Clement VIII. The pope refused because of political enmeshment; so in 1529, the king called into session the Parliament that was to declare the English Church independent of Rome. This animosity was present during the reign of Queen Elizabeth of England, but it will prove to be the turning point in Biblical prophecy.

Open trade with the united colonies, under King Philip II, was denied by the Queen. This forced merchants to become armed smugglers and pirates and made England a militant sea power. Religion added bitterness to the commercial rivalry. For years, Elizabeth's life was in constant danger from Spanish-Catholic plots, which perpetuated in England an undying hatred of papal Spain. Early in 1580, King Philip began planning to send a fleet to invade England. With financial support from the Vatican, he began to assemble what came to be known as the Armada. It consisted of 130 ships, but many lacked guns and experienced gunmen. It was the combined effort of *The Netherlands, Spain and France*. The defeat by England was a great blow to the prestige of Spain and the Vatican, but was instrumental in launching Great Britain to the rank of the seventh or last head of the wild beast. She became the greatest empire the world has yet seen. It did "devour the whole earth" in that "the sun never set" upon its possessions and territories.

Since Great Britain and Rome are both considered iron-like systems, according to the iron legs of Nebuchadnezzar's image, Daniel's prophecy pinpoints this notable occasion:

> Dan. 7:8 reveals the following: "I considered the horns, and behold there came up among them another horn, a little one, before which three [Armada] of the first horns were plucked up by the roots."

The British Empire developed as an imperialistic power. In time, the thirteen American colonies revolted against this seventh head. The government of the United States of America really was an extension of the iron-type rule and eventually became a close confederate to the British government. For hundreds of years, the monarch held most authority; however, as Parliament's power grew, the monarch's powers diminished.

By the beginning of the twentieth century, the peoples of Europe had reached an unprecedented level of comfort and civilization. The belief that the world was moving towards unity seemed to be growing in strength, despite the militant and nationalist movements of the time. This ascending process of civilized progression was suddenly interrupted by a crime.

On June 28, 1914, Archduke Franz Ferdinand, heir to the Austrian throne, was shot by Gavrilo Princip, a young fanatic of Sarajevo. A storm of indignation swept through Austria-Hungary, where it was believed by many that the crime was the work of the Black Hand and connived by officials of the Serbian government. The Kaiser was naturally fired with anger at the crime because he was a personal friend of the Archduke.

The stunning news that Europe was at war produced a

chaotic reaction throughout the world. The Germans, part of the sixth head of the wild beast, regarded themselves as the exponents of the highest form of civilization as yet attained. Rather than allow England, their ally, to go down, America would give up her long-cherished aversion for foreign entanglements. Ultimately, the consequences of America's entry into the war proved to be decisive. But on November 11, 1918, the firing suddenly ceased as rapidly as it began. The long and hideous nightmare was at last to an end. The treaties of peace were made under the direction of Wilson, Clemenceau and Lloyd George. In this scene of confusion, the American President at the opening of the conference was presented with the lustre of a Messiah. Although Germany was committed to a course of retribution, every effort was made to revive or *heal her wound* as foretold nearly 2,000 years ago:

> "One of its heads seemed to have a mortal wound, but its mortal wound was healed, and the whole earth followed the beast with wonder . . . " (Revelation 13:3, 4).

In the book, *The Late Great Planet Earth*, the author states that "many people have not known just what to make of this statement. . . . Whoever the person is with this fatal wound, will have a statue made of himself."

This is conjecturable nonsense. The meaning is clear and precise and in no way could logically apply to anything else. When an individual or council relies on preconceived traditions, the meanings become uncertain and unreliable. After revealing the "death stroke that was healed," it asserts in the fourth verse that "men worshipped the dragon for he had given authority to the beast." The Bible does not isolate nations but says "the whole world is lying in the power of the wicked one." There is no exception. In further reflections of the thirteenth chapter of Revelation, a startling reality will surface as the nations of the earth are being gathered to the day the lion roars.

70

Prophet of Delusion

Before considering the innovated "two horned beast" of Revelation and the "image" that was created as a false hope for mankind, a reinactment of Nebuchadnezzar's dream will reveal a clue to their identity:

Dan. 2:41-43 reads, "And as you saw the feet and toes partly of potter's clay and partly of iron, it shall be a divided kingdom, but some of the firmness of iron shall be in it. And as the toes of the feet were partly iron and partly clay, so the kingdom shall be partly strong and partly brittle. As you saw the iron mixed with miry clay, so they will mix with the seed of men."

After the wound was inflicted upon Germany during the Great War, two visible political organizations have been impending most remarkably before the wild beast. It has been Great Britain and the United States as an Anglo-American system. They exist as separate nations; however, they function as a dual world power in all aspects. They speak the same language, their heritage is identical, their principles and policies are the same, and they have been united ever since they resolved their differences in the War of 1812. The Monroe Doctrine of 1823 made this a coalition empire as exemplified during the First and Second World Wars.

This British-American dual power, according to Daniel's first dream, was an outgrowth of the head of the "fourth terrible beast." *It was a product of Rome.* Therefore, they would be represented by the feet of iron and clay—a power "partly strong and partly brittle." This dual system was the mightiest in human history and stronger than any of the preceding six world powers, but it had a weakness.

The number "ten," as previously examined, indicates an earthly completeness. It exhibits remnants of all powers and governments coexisting in this time of the end. Al-

71

though they are coexisting, they remain divided as the prophecy proclaims. From the Great War until the conclusion of this age, *there has never been nor will there ever be* an empire that will totally dominate the world. The nuclear generation allows many nations first strike capability, thus diminishing such claims.

Secondly, the feet are mixed with the "seed of men." The war against the German machine ended in a radical and revolutionary peace, drawn up by democratic politicians. It recognized the liberation of nations and canonized new policies to provide for the protection of the populus. The general trend was toward nationalism and democracy. It caused the mixing of the "seed of men" into the political structure, thus weakening its ruling element. It would mean socializing the forms of government and providing a political offspring.

From this new conception, a strong spirit of reform swept through the United States and Great Britain. Many reformers called for changes in economic, political and social systems. They wanted to reduce poverty, improve the living conditions of many, and regulate big business. They wanted a restraint on government corruption and know that a greater response be given to the citizens according to their needs. The progressive era criticized the school system and the various injustices in the society. It brought about labor unions and an increase in unskilled workers, resorting to strikes to gain concessions. This would often end up in violence and produce a chaotic climate. For certain, the "seed of men" has aimed at weakening and overthrowing the capitalist illusion, whereas democratic elements have weakened the power of the imperial, absolute monarchs, thus leading the nations to their inevitable demise. The Bible inferred that "men would become faint out of fear and expectation of the things coming upon the inhabited earth; for the powers of the heavens will be shaken."—(Luke 21:26).

John's vision now unmasks the role of the Anglo-

American dual power in the "time and seasons which the Father has fixed by his own authority."

> "Then I saw another beast which rose out of the earth; it had two horns like a lamb and it spoke like a dragon. It exercised all the authority of the first beast in its presence . . . " (Revelation 13:11, 12).

Daniel's first vision of the terrible beast adds for clarification that "the horn which had eyes and a mouth spoke great things." Since the first "wild beast" only consisted of seven political heads, the two-horned beast could not be regarded as an eighth head. Rather, it is another representation of the seventh head. The "two horns" typify a dual power [Anglo-American], and because it originated from the "earth" its presence came from an existing world power and not the "sea" of mankind. Daniel signified that the Anglo-American political combination showed concerned "eyes" for every situation that occurs in every corner of the earth and a mouth to magnify its own achievements. Their concern for the world shows them to be as fearful as a "lamb." However, from the fact that they "spoke like a dragon" discloses why they are fitly termed "false prophets," for it served as a spokesman for the entire wild beast.

Do not be misled into thinking that this false prophet is an individual such as the Jewish False Prophet, interpreted by many in the Biblical speculative arena. It is joined by the dragon and wild beast at Revelation 16:13 and undeniably identified as the two-horned beast at Revelation 19:20, where the false prophet is depicted as having the same function on earth as the two-horned beast. The froglike expressions or propaganda that comes from the mouth of the false prophet makes it clearly evident that it is an outstanding governmental system that takes upon itself the role of a prophet. The British-American powers took the lead in setting up an "image" to the beast and predicted great things in the interest of world peace.

The Illegitimate Image

At the close of World War I in 1918, the united political program for the postwar world was proposed. The American President Woodrow Wilson and British Prime Minister Lloyd George inspired and advocated the establishment of a League of Nations. The importance of the League is that it offered to the world as much world-government as the world could stand. It was to be altogether different from other ineffective manifestations. It was to be a permanent organ supported by all nations of the world for the transaction of international affairs and peace. It was an "image to the wild beast" in that it was the embodiment of every civilization that had ever existed. It couldn't have received God's blessing because it was made up of every religious credence in the world including atheism. It was an apparition divided against itself and was destined to fail.

Likewise, Daniel spoke of it as "the transgression that makes desolate." This was also reiterated in Matthew 24:15 as a factor of the composite sign pointing to the end of the world [aion]. In the apostle's day, it was the Roman army under General Titus that destroyed the temple and stood literally in the holy place. The Jewish cry of allegiance, "we have no king but Caesar," still sounds out today where, once again, the political illegitimate image prevails. The Federal Council of Churches of Christ stated that the League was the political expression of the kingdom of God on earth. The same corroboration was given by the Pope of Rome as well as religious leaders throughout the inhabited earth. In a time when the King, Christ Jesus, should be spiritually influencing the thoughts of man, the weak and beggarly elements of the world are still turning to man-made abominations for salvation.

In 1939, the League of Nations and the hope for peace ended in despair. However, this was predicted as well as a revival of the old format.

The Eighth Power

On April 25, 1945, forty-six nations sent delegates to the conference at San Francisco, California, to draw up the charter of the United Nations. It entered into force on October 24, 1945, when China, France, the U.S.S.R., the United Kingdom, the United States and a majority of other signatories had deposited their endorsement. The terms of the charter involving security were based on the assumption that it was possible for the five permanent members to agree on important questions. It was realized that should the Big Five fail to agree, the council would be unable to perform its functions. The growing animosity between the Soviet Union and the Western Powers resulted in frequent use of the veto which reduced the effectiveness of the Security Council.

The United Nations has two main goals, peace and human dignity. In numerous ways, the UN resembles the League of Nations. Many of the nations that founded the UN had also founded the League; however, there are two main differences. First, the UN has at its disposal military forces, and second, the UN's concern with economic and social problems gives it broader responsibility. It becomes as an eighth power within itself, but since there is no place for the development of another head, it clearly shows that *there will be no new world power* as predicted by many. The apostle John vividly clarifies the transition:

> "And there are seven kings: five have fallen [Egypt, Assyria, Babylon, Medo-Persia and Greece], one is [Rome], the other has not yet arrived [Anglo-American system], but when he does arrive, he must remain a short while. And the wild beast [the image] that was, but is not [League of Nations], is also an eighth king [United Nations], but springs from the seven [seven-headed beast], and it goes off into destruction" (Revelation 17:10, 11).

The accuracy of this occurrence in history is somewhat phenomenal. Conditions on earth, from man's attempt to rule man, have never been more perilous. Anarchy and violence continue unrestrained, and even from the worldly viewpoint, the present march of nations are nearing their end. However, we stand on the threshold of another major event in the history of mankind—the "great tribulation" which will culminate in the Battle of Armageddon.

Chapter 5
Lawless One Revealed

. . . Do not believe every inspired expression, but test the expression to see whether they originate with God.

1 John 4:1

Until the formation of the Italian kingdom, Rome was the capital of the Roman Empire. It was founded by Romulus about 753 B.C. At the time of Emperor Augustus, the first of the emperors who died 14 A.D., the population of the city was estimated to have been at least 1,300,000, and during the time of Emperors Vespasian and Trajan, it was surmised to have contained nearly 2,000,000 inhabitants.

Rome's form of religion and priesthood have been that of pagan origin. Many of the rituals of divination can be traced back to Babylonian, Persian and Grecian doctrine and practices. Their religion simulated a simple mode of life. The average Roman was interested in two things—abundant crop harvest and the welfare of his home. Roman theology had little connection with morality, and concepts of future life were very vague. Their belief was a kind of bargaining with the gods. To protect the family, they made offerings to the spirit of Vesta, whose realm was the hearth; to Janus, who watched over the doorway, and to the tutelary deities, who guarded the store house.

In addition to the spirits that offered protection to the family, there also those that safeguarded the state. These gods became more and more significant until a sort of public religion was generated, an official cult which stressed the citizens' duty to the state and also aimed at securing for the nation the fortunes of war and the destiny of the universe. The most influential of the deities was Jupiter, who controlled the physical universe; Mars, the god of war, and Tellus, the female goddess of fertility.

Rome cared little about the religion of her subjects. Even if she had, it is doubtful if she would have heard of the religious excitement in Palestine near the little town of Capernaum toward the close of the reign of Tiberius. An unfamiliar teacher had arisen among the Jews and was journeying about the country preaching a new doctrine that God was a universal, loving and forgiving father, and that love conquers all things.

In the thirty-third year of his life when Jesus and his disciples had come to Jerusalem for the celebration of the Feast of the Passover, the Pharisees, led by the high priest Caiaphas, accused him of sedition. He was arrested, tried and convicted. Pontius Pilate, the Roman governor, doubted the guilt of Jesus, but he confirmed the sentence of death in order to keep peace among the Jews. Jesus was then lead away and crucified, according to the Roman custom.

Within twenty years after the death of the Messiah, Christianity had been carried throughout Palestine and Syria and into the more distant provinces, even beyond the confines of the empire.

The Christian would tolerate no other gods, would not participate even in the most formal way the rites of the official or other religions, and vigorously condemned all other cults. This aroused the resentment of pagans of all types, accustomed as they were to living side by side, recognizing in one another's religion the worship of the same divine power. Christian ethics and morals, difficult though they were for the pagans to accept, bore fruit that could not be ignored. The pagans could also see that they had peace of mind, hope, and a certainty which was strong enough to carry them through the pains of persecution.

What is clearly apparent is that the teaching of Jesus was a prophetic one that began with the Hebrew prophets.

It was not priestly—it had no dedicated temple and no altar. It had no rites and ceremonies. The organization was very simple with the congregation meeting in homes of their brethren. *No distinction between laymen and clergy was recognized.* Each congregation had a number of elders or overseers whose functions were to preside over the meetings, discipline those not adhering to the teachings, and dispense charity.

The most serious specific charges brought against the Christians were that they were stubborn and consistent lawbreakers and that they refused to perform the duties of a citizen toward the government, and these charges were well-founded. The Christian could not accept public office, serve in the army or share in certain idolistic ceremonies. He felt that he owed his first homage to a higher source of supremacy than the worldly empire. The Christians were eventually thought of as anarchists contemplating on destroying the state.

Early Apostasy

As long as the Christian congregations were under the direct supervision of the apostles, errors and apostasies were not very common. The apostles knew that perversions of the truth would occur but still endeavored to build up the organization as a bulwark against such infiltration. In lieu of their efforts, there were tendencies which rapidly developed into dangerous departures from the faith. The causes of these were the insistence of some who had come over from Judaism to deny the development of Christianity. On the other hand, heathen philosophy and morals were mingled with Christian belief and practiced by some, and the result was the rise of corrupt or immoral sects.

In the year 56 A.D., a meeting was arranged by the apostle Paul at Ephesus. He gave his farewell to the elders gathered there and forewarned them of dangers that would be present after his departure:

"I know that after I leave, savage wolves will come in among you and will not spare the flock. Even from your own number, men will arise and distort the truth in order to draw away disciples after them" (Acts 20:25-31).

Paul died about ten years later. In his letters to Timothy just before his death, he repeatedly warned his fellow worker of the apostasy and gave him strong exhortation to exert himself forcefully because:

"The time will come when men will not put up with sound doctrine. Instead, to suit their own desires, they will gather around them a great number of teachers to say what their itching ears want to hear. They will turn their ears from the truth and turn aside to myths" (2 Timothy 4:3, 4).

The first century Christian congregations suffered much persecution from the "seed" of Satan. For nearly a century, the Christian lived in an unenviable state of suspense and insecurity, with Rome blowing hot and cold, as the political interest of the moment seemed to dictate. In spite of violent mistreatment, Christianity spread to the entire then-known world. Never in history has a threat developed of such magnitude against Satan's efforts to achieve religious domination. Determined to use a more cunning strategy, he planted weeds or imitation Christians among the wheat as foretold by Jesus. This proved to be a devastating maneuver to be experienced even in the time of the end. It would eventually produce a "lawless one."

By using the fundamental facts of farming, Jesus introduced a parable that does much to explain the history of Christianity throughout the centuries. It also speaks unquestionably of what was to occur after the "sleep" [death] of the apostles. They pleaded with him to "explain the illustration of the weeds in the field."

A farmer [the son of man] worked extremely hard in

sowing a crop of good wheat [sons of the kingdom] at seedtime and is quite convinced that when the harvest arrives it will be fruitful. But in time, the farm workers reported that his field was also producing weeds [apostate Christians], *a weed that was difficult to distinguish from the wheat.* He immediately thought of foul play from an enemy [Satan]. He had to make a decision in an effort to save the good crop. His employees suggested he uproot the weeds right away, but the farmer considered them too eager. Wisely, he told them to hold off for fear of uprooting the wheat. He informed them to let both grow together until the harvest season [time of the end], and then the wheat could be separated and stored in the barn [God's provisions], and the weeds will be collected and burned [Armageddon] (Matthew 13:36-42).

As previously stated, the tendencies away from the pure Gospel, as preached by Christ and the apostles, began to produce the admixture of Judaism, Christianity and the pagan elements. Apostatized divisions were already evident and by the end of the second century had defined their doctrine throughout the world. It was only natural that each independent church should be anxious to establish its "apostolic succession," and each was convinced that it alone was the legitimate heir to the special powers entrusted to Christ's church.

To fully comprehend the revolting counterfeit as being no ordinary enemy, but one which kept persistently trying to rear its head, we can look at a point made by the apostle John at the close of the first century. He wrote:

"Dear children, this is the last hour; and as you have heard that the antichrist is coming, even now many antichrists have come. This is how we know it is the last hour. They went out from among us, but they did not really belong to us. For if they had belonged to us, they would have remained with us;

but their going showed that none of them belonged to us" (I John 2:18, 19).

There has never been a word so aimlessly misused than the term "antichrist." It can be found in two of John's letters written just before his death in Ephesus. It appears only five times, and yet, religious leaders "have gone beyond the things written" and misapplied the meaning to unrelated texts.

In his book, *The 1980's, Countdown to Armageddon*, Hal Lindsey stretches his imaginative scholarship and states that "the anti-Christ will achieve the top spot in Europe on the strength of his own personality. But he will need the help of the Jewish false prophet. . . . "

World victory by any nation or individual man by the use of sheer peaceful diplomacy is absolute nonsense. The long-existing world governments are too observant to allow such a deceitful scheme to be put over on them. Contrary to such a belief, *there will be no individual antichrist* who will dominate the world without conflict. The inspired Scriptures are very clear as to the definition.

John indicates there are many antichrists and his use of the expression "hour" can mean a relatively short time or an undetermined length. Therefore, it does not restrict the appearance and existence of such antichrists to some future time only. It has been misapplied to Pompey, Nero, Mohammed and even the papacy. If one will observe, the term broadly embraces *all those* who deny that "Jesus is the Christ" and deny him "to be the Son of God who came in the flesh" (Compare Luke 11:23). It would include all "false Christs" and "false prophets." It would embrace those who persecute followers of Christ or those who claim they "perform powerful works in His name." The expression, "those who went out from us," ties vividly to the phrase the apostle Peter used to denounce the apostates. What about the "Lawless One," "the man of sin," "the son of perdition"? The Lawless One can be identified as an antichrist;

however, the antichrist is not the Lawless One. The great anti-Christian apostasy can now be revealed.

The Man of Lawlessness

After the death of Christ's apostles and their close associates, there came a period of the Congregation's struggle with the combined forces of the pagan state, pagan philosophy and culture, and the inherent opposition of sin. This apostasy, previously disclosed, is to result in the revealing of "the man of lawlessness." As the old pagan Roman Empire decayed, there grew in its midst a new spiritual empire.

Among the many forms of apostate organizations, the Church of Rome was occupying the most prominent place. This was attributed to the fact that it was found essentially within the empire. The popularity of other Christianized sects such as Gnosticism, the Montanist movement and the Marcionite churches forced others, including the Church of Rome, to refine and formulate their beliefs. The Catholic Church [the term first known from an early letter of Ignatius] favored three motives to procure unification. One was the desire to unite all believers into a fellowship. A second proposal was to maintain and disperse the Gospel in its purest form, and the final suggestion was in creating a visible body of Christ. However, it proved to be disastrous because in the process of defining the faith and in developing an organization, contradictions arose and animosity manifested itself. Those who considered themselves to be Christians separated into other organizations and excommunicated one another.

The Church endeavored to deal with the predicament by developing a solution that sticks with them to this day. First, they ascertain lines of bishops who were *assumed* to be in direct or uninterrupted succession from the apostles. This would produce the *theory* of apostolic succession. Secondly, because the bishops were becoming exceedingly prominent as essential features of the Church, a *clergy-laity distinction* began to appear. By the end of the second century, the clergy had clearly become a separate order that was probably from the designation given to Roman magistrates. *It clearly was maneuvered in direct opposition to God.*

The great apostasy was not something that happened with unexpectedness. It developed in a very deceitful manner. The apostles were clearly warned of the manifestation that was to take place from the example set by the Jewish leaders. Jesus' words were explicit:

> "All the works they do they do to be viewed by men; They like the most prominent place at evening meals and the front seats in the synagogues, and the greetings in the marketplaces and to be called Rabbi by men. But you, do not be called Rabbi, for one is your teacher, whereas all you are brothers. Moreover, do not call anyone your father on earth for one is your Father, the heavenly One. Neither be called leaders, for your leader is one, the Christ. . . . Whoever exalts himself will be humbled, and whoever humbles himself will be exalted" (Matthew 23:5-12).

There were a number of men in the early congregation that took advantage of their position of responsibility. They thought of themselves with ascribed importance and even demanded special privileges. They seduced and misdirected many with their counterfeit words (2 Corinthians 11:19, 20). Gradually, under the influence of the pagan mystery religions of Babylon, Persia and the Hellenic civilization, the ritual of Christianity increased to such a stage of complexity that a professional priesthood was necessary. Let's consider Paul's warning of this "son of destruction":

> "Let no one seduce you in any manner, because it will not come unless the apostasy comes first and

the man of lawlessness gets revealed, the son of destruction. He is set in opposition and lifts himself up over everyone who is called 'god' or an object of reverence, so that he sits down in the temple of The God, publicly showing himself to be a god. Do you remember that, while I was yet with you, I used to tell you these things? And so now you know the thing that acts as a restraint [apostles], with a view to his being revealed in his own due time. True, the mystery of this lawlessness is already at work; but only till he who is right now acting as a restraint [apostles] gets to be out of the way [their death]. Then, indeed, the lawless one will be revealed, whom the Lord Jesus will do away with by the Spirit of his mouth and bring to nothing by the manifestation of his presence [the great tribulation]. But the lawless one's presence is according to the operation of Satan with every powerful work and lying signs and portents and with every unrighteous deception for those who are perishing, as a retribution because they did not accept the love of the truth . . . " (2 Thessalonians 2:3-12).

Notice that Paul personifies the great Christian apostate as the "man of lawlessness." It would be impossible to make reference to the lawless one as an individual and not a collective man. *He was already at work in Paul's day* and would be destroyed at the presence of the Lord Jesus. This would make him nearly 2,000 years old and reflect another absurdity of modern interpreters. Moffatt's translation of the verb form at 1 Timothy 4:1 reads: "Certain people will rebel against the faith." It is evident that he is against the Most High God because he tries to exalt himself over everything that is called god. God's Word will gradually be substituted by a Christian religion fused with traditions and pagan thoughts.

The Church of Rome was becoming stronger and more popular and ultimately came to embody elements from a wide variety of sources. It was also more belligerent to the government and hence more dangerous. The last and most thorough attempt to stamp it out began in 303 A.D. by Diocletian, the great reformer and was continued by his successors until 311 A.D.

The resignation of Diocletian in 305 A.D. was followed by years of bitter strife. By 312 A.D. there were four rival emperors, one of whom was Constantine the Great. His military position was very uncertain against Licinius and Maxentius. Gathering his legions together, Constantine marched swiftly into Italy staking his entire career on the chance of victory against superior forces. It was at this time that he decided to seek the support of the Church of Rome. At any rate, to that period belongs the story so variously interpreted of his vision of a fiery cross in the sky and the words, *Hoc vince* [by this conquer] which he took as his emblem. From that time on, Constantine became steadily more favorable with the Christianized apostate religion.

That Constantine's policy was inspired to any great degree by religious motives seems most unlikely. He was evidently lured toward the idea of monotheism, as were many knowledgeable pagans, but his workings were that of a profound and farsighted statesman rather than a convert. Although his change was apparent, the purpose of Constantine was still indistinct. He believed in Christ but also in the unconquered sun. He tolerated Christians but retained the office of Pontifex Maximus. His coins bore the emblem of Christianity on one side, and on the other side an attestation to sun worship. Yet when the pagan emperor had completed his journey, the Church of Rome became the sole official religion of the empire.

Christianity in its complete development sought to establish a dynasty. With this extreme acceptance of the Roman Church in mind, one has to revert back to the time when Jesus was impelled to retire into the wilderness of

Judea for forty days. After Jesus fasted and communed with his Father, Satan placed before him three temptations. The third and final enticement was the climatic one. He offered him "all the kingdoms of the world and their glory." Jesus did not deny that the adversary could rightly give all authority and glory of them for a simple act of worship, but he rejected the offer to gain earthly domination. However, nearly three centuries later, a reoccurrence of the same attempt took place. Are we to assume that Jesus reconsidered and now authorized an offer of human rulership in conjunction with the political government to be made to the bishops of Rome? Are we to imply that Jesus Christ, from heaven, was offering such "bishops" a dynasty that he had refused? Secular eccesiastical history answers unequivocally *No!* If, upon accepting Christianity as a state religion, Constantine thought of the text, "My kingdom is no part of this world," he must have allowed himself an asquint smile.

From the beginning of his reign, Constantine tried to help the Church by granting special privileges to the bishops. He apparently intended to act as the embodiment of the Church to the non-Christian population of the empire, even to the extent of calling himself "bishop." The transfer of wealth to the Church and the exemption of the Church from taxation threw greater responsibility on the rest of the people. The chief burden of taxation fell on the land. When a farmer was unable to pay his taxes, they were collected from his neighbors. It developed into a type of manorialism with the people dependent on the Church for protection from enemies, for justice, and for what tolerable government that was available.

The rapid growth of the Church was not all pure gain. The inflow of great numbers of the incurious consequently lowered the general average of morality and religious zeal while at the same time introducing non-Christian elements into its doctrine and practice. It became an organism that fed upon the whole pagan world, selecting and incorporating a wide variety of practices which were not consistent with the early congregation.

The easy conversion of those who were merely following the course of least resistance signified no vital change in their method of life or thought. They clung to ancient superstitions as the Church translated them into terms of the new religion. The cult of saints and martyrs sprung up to take the place of the many gods of pagan mythology. The pagan could rely upon the adoption of a patron saint for his protection and simple requests. Christian celebrations were created to replace pagan feasts and holidays. For example, the date of Christmas *which had no connection with the birth of Christ* was set on the birthday of Mithras [the unconquered sun]. The observance of the Jewish Sabbath was transferred to the Mithraic Sun-day and the worship of Mary in the tenor of Isis, the Queen of Heaven. And finally, the custom and symbols associated with the observance of Easter [Eostre or Astarte] have ancient origins in the rites of fertility.

The Nicene Farcical

During the second and third centuries, many doctrinal differences interrupted the peace within the Church of Rome. In the time of Constantine, everything pertaining to the affairs of the Church became endowed with supreme importance. The protest over Arius, a deacon from Alexandria, threatened to disrupt the entire structure of the new Roman apostasy. Arius began by a controversy with a clergyman named Bausalas, in which the eternal existence of the Son of God was the subject of dispute. The matter became notorious, and the bishop was driven to take some steps respecting it. He called together a synod composed of a hundred of the neighboring bishops to hear what each of the disputants had to say. The assembly decided that the doctrine of Arius was not the doctrine of the Church. The assembly condemned him.

The substance of the Arian doctrine may be stated in a few words. It is that although the second person in the Trinity may be designated as God, he is not the Almighty God because he is not eternal, and therefore, there was a time when he did not exist. Even after the condemnation by the bishops and the provincial council, Arius left the city and went throughout all Palestine endeavoring to obtain support for his teaching.

The conflict threatened to divide the Church in the eastern region of the empire. The bishops immediately called upon the pagan emperor to settle the doctrinal dispute regarding the Trinity. Constantine summoned the first Ecumenical Council at Nicaea in 325 A.D. All the bishops were invited; however, only 318 came. Along with their attendants, the gathering numbered over 2,000.

On the arrival of Constantine, the council was formally opened. Would it surprise or even shock some to know that the very foundation of their religion was formulated without the presence or approval of the Bishop of Rome? It's true. First, an address to the emperor was recited by Eusebius along with a thanksgiving to God for the emperor's victory of war over Licincus. Then, from his throne Constantine addressed the assembly. Coming to the main purpose for which the council was collected, Arius rose to speak whereupon the assembled bishops raised their hands and closed their ears. Nicholas of Myra struck him in the face then ran out. Arius was expelled, and the council set themselves to issue the result of their deliberation in the form of the Nicene Creed. *The emperor gave his final approval* and issued a letter sent throughout all the empire that the decisions of the council were to be enforced with the penalty of death for disobedience. Constantine died in the year 337 A.D., being baptized only three days before his death. However, the Arian controversy was not weakened to the point of deactivation until the second Ecumenical Council of Constantinople. As predicted by the actions of the Lawless One, he has nearly reached the pinnacle of his power when he "sits down in the temple . . . showing himself to be a god." From this point on, he will display himself in dissimilar forms but each time exalting himself to be seen by men. Perhaps as much as anything that caused the Church of Rome to win over Arius, and that will be prevalent throughout history is that the former were ever ready *to resort to violence* and force their will if necessary. It's ironic to think that the fundamental structure of Christendom today was based on the decision of an unbaptized pagan emperor whose hands were full of innocent blood, including that of his wife and son. Where is the *aga'pe love* that once shrouded the early Christian congregation?

Post-Nicene Vendetta

An institution that is inhuman and deceitful cannot produce righteous men. By examining the papacy in view of historical facts, it will become evident that it was conceived in a fraudulent and counterfeit character. Every involvement in its growth was in variance of the Scriptures, and its intentions were always worldly and completely political. All popes cannot be said to have been common criminals; however, the pursuit of wealth and power, the buying and selling of ecclesiastical favors, the enrichment of their offsprings and relatives, and the preservation of fraudulent practices can be proven against almost every pope who existed.

Ideas of worldly domination by the Church were already prevalent in the fourth century. Saint Augustine, one of the greatest leaders of the Church, asserted in his book, *The City of God,* that the aim of the organization was to make the world into a theological and organized Kingdom of Heaven. And in time, the Church was to be the ruler of the entire world. After the barbarian struggles were settled, the bishop began to claim an overlordship over their kings.

From this point on, events moved rapidly. The bishops

in all the provinces were assuming greater power. In many cities, they took over the duties of the imperial government acting as judges and governors. With these added responsibilities, they were forced to look for a greater authority for moral support and guidance.

The first pope who seemed to have perceived the great role after the disintegration of the Roman Empire was Leo the Great. He elevated the Bishop of Rome to a position of supremacy in the Latin Church comparable to that of the emperor. With the final fall of the Western Empire, he took over the ancient title of *Pontifex Maximus* and so became the supreme interpreter of sacred law.

As was previously defined, the "man of lawlessness" is a composite body of men; however, it can rightfully be reflected to all possessing such distinction as defined by Farraris' ecclesiastical dictionary:

> "The pope is of such dignity and highness that he is not simply a man but, as it were, God, and the Vicar of God. . . . Hence the pope is crowned with a triple crown, as king of heaven, of earth and of hell. . . . Nay, the pope's excellence and power are not only about heavenly, terrestrial and infernal things, but he is also above angels, and is their superior. . . . So that if it were possible that angels could err in faith, or entertain sentiments contrary thereto, they could be judged and excommunicated by the pope. . . . He is of such great dignity and power that he occupies one and the same tribunal with Christ. . . . So that whatsoever the pope does seems to proceed from the mouth of God. . . . The pope is, as it were, God on earth, the only prince of the faithful of Christ, the greatest king of all kings, possessing the plenitude of power; to whom the government of the earthly and heavenly kingdom is entrusted. . . . The pope is of

such great authority and power that he can modify, declare or interpret the divine law. . . . The pope can sometimes counteract the divine law, etc."

The "man of lawlessness" has always had the idea that he had the right to rule over others and that those ruling in his midst were kings or rulers by divine right. Notice the apostle, Paul's, words at I Corinthians 4:8:

"Already you have all you want! Already you have become rich! You have become kings—and that without us! How I wish that you really had become kings so that we might be kings with you."

These words have been completely ignored as the following symposium of compromise, political influence and power, bitterness, divisions and bloodshed depict:

476 A.D. Odovacar, leader of the barbarian soldiers from beyond the Danube, made up the greater part of the Roman army in Italy. He decided to do away with the puppet emperor Romulus Augustulus and took the government outright for himself. The Roman Empire was theoretically united once more under one emperor. Rather than depending upon the spirit of God to anoint, the Church readily accepted the domination of the Roman emperors.

483 A.D. Bishop Felix of Nantes was appointed by Odovacar as Pope Felix III. The division between the Eastern and Western churches was widened after the pope excommunicated Acacius, the Patriarch of Constantinople. The schism ended in 519 A.D.

488 A.D. The appointment of Pope Gelasíus I was ratified by the emperor. Gelasíus formulated what

was to be called the Gelasian theory, or the conception of church-state relations.

489 A.D. After thirteen years of uninterrupted rule in Italy, Odovacar found his position threatened by a new barbarian invasion. The Emperor Zeno sought to rid himself of a dangerous ally and commissioned Theodoric to invade Italy and repress Odovacar. Having victimized Odovacar into negotiating a peace treaty, he assassinated him and completed his conquest of Italy.

493 A.D. After the death of Odovacar, Theodoric appointed popes Symmachus, Hormisdas, John I and Felix IV. Justinian, the Byzantine regent, issued a proclamation banishing all pagans and heretics, including the Arians and Manicheans, from the empire. The Arians implored Theodoric to protect them. The emperor asked Pope John I to go to Constantinople and intercede, but the pope protested. With Theodoric's persistence, John left for the city but returned without accomplishing his goal. Theodoric accused him of treason and sentenced him to prison, where he died a year later. Meanwhile, Pope Symmachus had defended his son-in-law after being found guilty of a crime against the state. Symmachus himself was charged and arrested. His executioners tied a cord around his head and tightened it until his eyes burst from their sockets. After a severe beating, he died. Shortly thereafter, Theodoric followed his victims to the grave.

526 A.D. Theodoric's grandson Athalaric was designated to succeed him. Being only ten years old, his mother Amalasuntha ruled in his name. She exposed the boy to Gothic tutors; he took to sexual permissiveness and died at eighteen. His mother appointed the first German pope, Boniface II.

Theodoric's son Theodatus appointed popes John II, Agapitus and Silverius.

537 A.D. Theodora was first, the mistress of Justinian, then his wife, and later, the Empress. Earlier, she grew up in a circus and shortly thereafter, became a prostitute. She practiced abortion with recurring success and eventually gave birth to an illegitimate child. Justinian fell in love with her. She took an active part in ecclesiastical politics, enthroning and dethroning popes at her leisure. She connived with Vigilus, Roman deacon, to make him pope if he would offer concession to the Monophysites, people named for their specific Christian religion of ancient Egypt. Pope Silverius was bodily removed from the throne and exiled to the island of Palmaria where he died from severe treatment. Vigilus was made pope by the orders of the emperor. Never had emperors so openly endeavored to dominate the papacy.

590 A.D. Gregory I [the Great] had accomplished much in the unity of the Catholic Church; however, he was superstitious and physically crazed with an overreligious piety. He was appointed pope with the approval of the emperor in Constantinople. The four popes preceeding him and the twenty-four that followed him, ending with Gregory II, required ratification from the monarchs.

651 A.D. An enormous amount of wealth began to sift into the Church's treasury. France proved to be the richest possession. The Merovingian kings, who were guilty of polygamy and murder, showered the bishops with monetary proceeds as well as land, being confident of buying their way into heaven. The newly converted Franks gave the Church their sanctimonious gifts that they had stolen from conquered peoples.

726 A.D. Emperor Leo III of Constantinople forbade the use of images in worship. Pope Gregory II excom-

municated him which lead to the separation of the Greek Church from the Latin Church.

795 A.D. Rome continued to decline with the municipal factions becoming less effective. The diversified populus, living in filth and misery, relieved the pressure by the practice of sexual perversions and self-righteous gifts to the papacy. The only way they had to express their political emotions were by frequent revolts against foreign monarchs or popes that didn't measure up to their expectations. The permanent noble families spent most of their leisure time competing with one another for control of the papacy. Since the election of the pope was now the responsibility of the Italian factions and not the emperor, it brought about what can be described as tortuous elections. The cohesive groups became so engrossed within themselves and with the general public, fighting was often commonplace, and occasionally, it ended in a blood bath with the pope elect the victim.

800 A.D. In an effort to exalt itself over the world rulers, the Roman Catholic Church interfered in the political arena by appointing Charlemagne over Irene, the empress of Constantinople. This established the "Holy Roman Empire" which survived until the year 1806.

828 A.D. The gulf between the rich and the poor enlarged as the rich became vastly richer. No mercy was shown, and many of the poor were sold as slaves to the Saracens. The pious profits were used to build shrines to the saints. Merchants of Venice had stolen what was believed to be relics of St. Mark. He became the patron saint of Venice, causing them to pillage much of Italy to enshrine the bones. Most of the relics were fraudulent, but it didn't matter to the mesmerized populus.

897 A.D. Popes now followed one another in rapid succession, as the various factions controlled Rome. Pope Formosus, after serving nearly five years, died of a stroke. The armed Roman citizens replaced him with Pope Boniface VI who died before the end of one year. Stephen VII, who was declared insane, sat on the throne for one year. He had the corpse of Pope Formosus exhumed, dressed it in a royal robe and tried the body before an ecclesiastic council on the charge of heresy. The corpse was condemned and dragged through the streets as the people screamed, threw stones and plunged it into the Tiber River. A revolution was in preparation the following year, and the pope was arrested and thrown into prison, where he was strangled.

904 A.D. Theophylact, a chief official of the papal palace, was influential in making or breaking popes at will. He had a daughter named Marozia who secured the office for her lover Sergius III. Likewise, his wife contrived for the appointment of Pope John X, believed to be her lover. Marozia lived according to her lustful desire and enjoyed a succession of lovers. With the aid of Guido, Duke of Tuscany, they unseated John and had him imprisoned, where he died from causes unknown. Marozia then raised up John XI to the papacy, known to be her bastard son, but her son Aberic imprisoned John and ruled Rome for nearly twenty-two years. After his death, Marozia's grandson became Pope John XII and disgraced the papacy with perverted orgies in the palace. John XII was summoned by Otto I of Germany to appear before the council for taking bribes to consecrate bishops. One such appointment was a boy of ten who had committed adultery with his father's concubine and incest with his father's widow and

niece. The council discharged him and elected a layman as Pope Leo VIII.

988 A.D. The Russian Queen, Olga, Grandduke and Vladimir I, received baptism on a visit to Constantinople. All his subjects were compelled to follow his example in lieu of punishment. Russian paganism did not vanish but was fused with their beliefs. This is found to be the case in many countries in the twentieth century.

1032 A.D. Early in the tenth century, the Church declared that the final century of history had begun and that the faithful should prepare for the Final Judgement. The majority gave no evidence of any panic or fear but continued on their course of debauchery. The papacy was no exception, and eventually, decay resumed. In the year 1032, Benedict IX was elected pope at the age of fourteen years. Because of his perverted life and his toying with the occults, he was forced to leave Rome. Through the Tusculan house he was restored but sold the throne to Gregory VI for one thousand pounds of gold. Gregory's reforms were too severe so a third faction set up Sylvester III. The Italian clergy appealed to emperor Henry III to intercede. He came to Sutri, near Rome and set up an ecclesiastical council. Sylvester was imprisoned, Benedict resigned and Gregory was disposed of for admittedly purchasing the papacy. The Bishop of Bamberg was elected as Clement II; however, he died a year later. After Damasus II succumbed to malaria, Pope Leo IX finally resolved the deplorable condition to normality.

1098 A.D. We need to say very little about the Crusades. They were not for the purpose of retrieval or safeguarding the Holy Places in Palestine. It was to whom the popes adjudged to be enemies that mass slaughter resulted. Because the military orders included vows of poverty, chasity, and obedience, it was labeled a Holy War. The massacre was terrible; the blood of the captives ran down the streets until men splashed in blood as they rode. The Children's Crusade of 1212 was the result of the enthusiastic appeals of medievalism. Many youths that responded ended up as slaves in Egypt.

1159 A.D. Pope Alexander III decreed that no one could make a valid will except in the presence of clergy. If a public notary violated this order, he was to be excommunicated and condemned to Purgatory.

1170 A.D. It was proclaimed by the Church that gifts and legacies were a sure means of breaking loose from the pains of Purgatory. Properties to the Church grew from century to century. It was not unusual for a monastery to own thousands of manors, several towns, or even a large city or two. At one time, half of Europe was owned by monasteries and other Church institutions.

1246 A.D. The attitude of the Church toward the treatment of Jews only added to the ordeals of Jewish life. The periodic councils inflicted tortuous restraints that would have appalled the early Christians. They were ordered to stay indoors during Holy Week and had to reschedule the Passover feast because it too often overlapped the Easter celebration. Christian doctors and nurses were prohibited to treat Jews, as they were classified with harlots and a source of pollution. Christian marriage to Jews was forbidden, with the death sentence imposed for violators. Many Jews were dragged into Churches and ordered to be baptized. If they refused, they were slain as they knelt. Their children were kidnapped and conveyed to schools where they were forcibly taught Catholicism.

1378 A.D. The Great Western Schism began. In 1309, Pope Clement V moved the papacy to Avignon,

France. Gregory XI, in 1377, reestablished it again in Rome. After his death, the clergy, as well as the populus, developed fear that the papacy would leave Rome, so the Italian Pope Urban VI was elected. The new pope soon showed himself to be quick-tempered and arrogant, and his reforms made the electing factions regret their choice. Several months had passed, and the cardinals chose another pope claiming that the previous election was invalid. Urban was labeled as an antichrist and Clement VII was appointed as the new pope. Clement, being French, returned the papacy to Avignon, and Urban continued to rule from Rome. Ecclesiastical factions took sides, and if one pope would excommunicate a man, the other would release him from the stigma. The Council of Constance met to alleviate the scandal, but instead of remedying matters elected a third pope, John XXIII. Through violence and interventions of civil powers, the council ended the schism.

1492 A.D. Into the game of Italian politics, the Church immerged in full array. The popes from Martin V to Innocent III were notorious in their determination to advance the fortunes of their children and to meet extravagant expenditures, even to the sale of their office. In 1492, Alexander VI [Rodrigo Borgia] emerged as pope, obtaining the office by bribing the cardinals. He brought the papacy to the lowest point of moral degradation since the tenth century. He had sired illegitimate children and sought to immortalize his first favorite mistress Rosa Vannozza. The churches of Rome are full of statues and paintings portraying popes, their mistresses, and their progeny. One bas-relief is the "Madona and Child" posed for by Rosa and her infant Valentino. During his eleven years as pope, Alexander VI achieved an astronomical amount of wealth through disguised robbery of nobles and ecclesiastics, a number of whom he caused to be assassinated or poisoned.

1510 A.D. Literally, the warlike Pope Julius II, forced Michelangelo to paint the Sistine frescoes. He refused twice, but only agreed the third time after there was a fear that the infuriated pope would invade the city of Florence with his army.

The Religious Insurrection

The inquisition was a tribunal in the Church of Rome for the trial and punishment of heretics. It has been vindicated by the papacy in our day by the "Syllabus" of 1864. The first foundation of it was laid by Pope Innocent III which resulted in the massacre of 30,000 persons of every age and sex. It was formally established under Pope Gregory IX in 1229. In the first eighteen years of the Inquisition, 10,220 prisoners were burned alive and 97,321 imprisoned, exiled or stripped of their property. In 1540, Pope Paul III, alarmed at the spread of the Lutheran doctrine, appointed a committee to search out the participants and administer punishment.

Henry VIII's divorce was the occasion of England's breach with Rome, but causes had been gathering for centuries before. The cry for reform, therefore, was general before the great revolution appeared.

On October 31, 1517, Luther's conflict with the Church of Rome began when he boldly attacked the doctrine of "Indulgences." He soon had to defend himself against the charge of insubordination. The result of this defiance was his excommunication by Pope Leo X. Eventually, the reformers entered into a covenant called the "Smalcald League," which embodied their principles and laid the foundation for protestantism.

The Christianized apostate Church of Rome had

ushered in the "man of lawlessness" and is guilty of treason against God by means of its paganized religious teachings and practices. It became a vicious deception that brought about more violent deaths than anything that man has ever fantasized.

There are questions concerning the Reformation that need to be answered and reactions that are essential to survival in this time of the end. What did it reform? Are they still embroiled with the political governments of the world and war that stain their skirts with blood? *Did it remove itself from the foundations of the collective man of lawlessness?* Let's continue with our panoramic view of insurrection:

1524 A.D. Several Protestant reformers wanted to return to the primitive Christianity of the first century. One such group rejected infant baptism and therefore were called "Anabaptist." They were bitterly persecuted by other Protestants because of upsetting the established order. In Zurich, they were arrested, tried and condemned to life imprisonment. The Catholic, Lutheran and Zwinglians joined forces to stamp them out. During this period, hundreds of Anabaptists were killed, some by drowning and others by burning at the stake.

1525 A.D. The general uprising of the downtrodden peasants, frequently joined by the discontented working classes, brought into existence the "Peasants War." Luther's assertion that the Bible is the only authority caused the lowly masses to demand justice and relief from social burdens. Luther was as much alarmed as the princes at the revolt. He warned the peasants to obey the magistrates. When they refused, he ordered the princes to crush and slay the army of peasants.

1534 A.D. The Catholic reformers began to receive some cooperation from the papacy. After the establishment of the "Society of Jesus" or "Jesuits," as they were called, the Counter-Reformers took on new vigor and crushed out all opposition from Protestantism in the lands it controlled. Under Pope Paul III, the Inquisition was to be reorganized in Italy.

1553 A.D. Michael Servetus was a scholar, a physician and a scientist. His contribution to society was in connection with the discovery of the pulmonary circulation system. He was deeply religious but would not accept the doctrines of the Trinity, predestination, or infant baptism. On his way to Switzerland, he was arrested, tried and burned at the stake for heresy with the approval of the Protestant reformer John Calvin.

1559 A.D. The Reformation came to France against the opposition of the monarchy. The Protestants were forced to organize the political-religious party known as the "Huguenots." Calvinism had gained steadily and became increasingly militant.

1562 A.D. The Protestants took arms to defend their faith and opened the "Wars of Religion" against the Catholic League. Fanatical mobs on both sides soon accounted for the massacre of thousands.

1585 A.D. Henry III was in feeble health and had no sons, and the nearest heir to the throne was now the Protestant Bourbon prince, Henry of Navarre, who was the most active leader of the Huguenots. Rather than accept him, the Catholic League was prepared to go to any length. The war that followed was called the "War of the Three Henrys." After the death of Henry III, Henry of Navarre proclaimed himself King of France as Henry IV. After four years and the slaughter of many, Henry decided to change coats and adopted the Catholic faith. The war ended.

1618 A.D. The revived energy of Catholicism and the

rising power of militant Calvinism tended to increase the tension and to produce a situation that menaced the peace of Europe. It was known as the "Thirty Years War." When it was over, Germany lay prostrate, and the Holy Roman Empire had been reduced to an empty shell. The war scattered death, disease and destruction in its wake, all for the religious control of territory, all in the name of Christianity.

1620 A.D. The Anglican Church remained the privileged state church of England and taught the doctrine that it was wicked to resist the king because he was ordained of God. It caused undue pressure upon the "Saints," a left wing group known to the public as "Separatists." Seeing no hope of purity in official doctrine, they formed a new organization of their own. In time, they boarded the Mayflower and sailed for the new world, erronously arriving at the northern tip of Cape Cod.

1630 A.D. The Puritans arrived and settled in Massachusetts. They immediately enacted all the ecclesiastical reforms which they were unable to produce in England. Like most Protestant revolutionaries, they exaggerated the importance of ideology, and the persecuted became the persecutors. Anyone not adhering to their interpretation of "law" and "grace" were either banished, strangled or hanged. The new distortions of Protestantism caused the most shocking episode in American history—the trial and execution of witches in Salem.

1861 A.D. The most far-reaching of the schisms in American churches occurred over Negro slavery. It split Methodism wide open in 1844 with the great Baptist split in 1845. The Presbyterian house divided right down the Mason-Dixon line. Completely separate religious organizations were established to conform to political and social reforms. When the Civil War began, prayers filled the airway to God for his nonpartisan support as they slaughtered each other. The Episcopalians did not divide— they just went out and shot, each one, his brother in the futility of nationalism.

1865 A.D. In the midst of unparalleled success, Abraham Lincoln was assassinated. Testimonies show that the Mary Surratt house on H Street, Washington, D.C., was the common rendezvous of John Wilkes Booth and prominent priests of the district. During the trial of "Surratt," it was surmised that Jefferson Davis had filled the mind and heart of Booth with fanatical religious patriotism and that the pope was the possible incentor.

1867 A.D. The Ku Klux Klan [members originally of southern church groups] were formed and devoted to the protection of womanhood and white Protestants from the Blacks.

To the great humiliation of the Protestant churches, religious intolerance and even persecution unto death were continued long after the Reformation. At first sight, Protestantism was a confused medley of sects which warred with one another and the Roman Catholic Church. Out of Protestantism arose democratic movements within both church and state; however, *there is nothing in the Protestant world that can be compared with the unity of the early Christian congregation.* It has only produced a crop of divided churches and sects—a system called "syncretism" or the mixing together of beliefs from different religions.

In 1888, William II [Kaiser Wilhelm] became chancellor of Germany. The Triple Alliance had been safely renewed. Since not only Italy, but also Austria-Hungary was Roman Catholic, it was only to be expected that the pope would favor the agreement. Because of an assassination within the borders of Christendom, World War I was touched off. By the end of the war, *there were twenty-four nations of Christendom* together with only four non-Christian countries that were fighting one another. Representatives of Britain and America argued for an international peace-keeping organization. The peace conference signed the treaty in which the covenant for a League of Nations had been incorporated. In 1919, religious organizations rallied in favor of the League, thus, adopting the worldly substitute for peace.

In 1933, Hitler's accession to power was endorsed. He could not repress a certain reluctant admiration for the Catholic Church. Like Mussolini before him, Hitler acknowledged the strategical advantage of coming to terms with Catholicism. The offer of an agreement was accepted and a concordant, negotiated by Msgr. Pacelli [Pope Pius XII], was signed in July of that year. The Church was assured of full religious freedom. In return, the Church ordered bishops to take an oath of loyalty to the Third Reich.

Relations with the Protestant churches was also a part of Hitler's illusion of world domination. His objective was to capture the governmental machinery of the twenty-eight territorial churches and create a united national church under a national bishop accepted by the party.

When World War II began, the national churches once again merged themselves in their respective warring nation. Pulpits were transformed into amateur recruiting offices, and the approval of violence becomes a farce. In a ritualistic mode, the clergy bless the troops and offer prayers for victory—while another group on the other side publicly pray for the opposite outcome. The devastating total of the two great wars came to 69 million idiotic killings. The nationalistic barriers of Christendom have resulted in the greatest contradiction of peace on earth.

Protestant Indulgences

The latest estimated number of religious groups into which humanity is divided are ten main religions, but there are over 10,000 churches and sects. It is interesting, however, that the greater number have all sprung up within the past thirty years. Certainly, the critical point that now prevails in churches provides much of the breeding ground for dissension, and understandably, the signs of the times have designated uneasiness.

Churches are concerned about a dwindling support and are making an effort to revive the emotional senses of their members. But their tactics result in the exploiting of a pleasure-oriented apprehension. Churches have become "Holy Ghost" entertainment centers. Many employ clowns who dance, juggle, mime or ride bicycles throughout the church. Other clergymen attract attendance with Karate demonstrations, magicians and even exotic dancers. It has produced contributions that prove to be disguised Protestant indulgences. The conferral for such religious slapstick entertainment assures the beneficiary a promenade to heavenly bliss.

The most precarious example of professional magnetism is the Electric Church or TV preachers who purchase their own air time and use it to obtain contributions with which to buy more air time. They utilize services of folk singers, astronauts, rock groups, movie stars and other celebrities to bolster their appeal. It has become a very profitable business with exorbitant sums of money being filtered into massive structural complexes. It has deepened the values of a materialistic consumer culture. It becomes a deceptive vice that promises easy salvation with one act of gratuity.

There can be little doubt that the Reformation caused a pungent shaking to the Roman Catholic Church; however, in reality it is only a by-product of Catholicism and has all the earmarks in many ways. It has not proven to be a restoration of Christianity as it existed before the great apostasy. Since the days of Luther, Protestantism has been adulterously allied with the political governments of the world, even to the extent of clergy participation in the presidential candidacy. They have been embroiled in wars, the members never vacillating to pick up the sword to kill those classed as political enemies although they may have been denominational brothers. And finally, they have maintained their clergy-laity distinction which is the true mark of the collective "Lawless One." Only a complete individual renewal will eradicate the token of infamy.

Chapter 6
Kings of Vexation

For there exists a time and judgement
even for every affair . . . calamity
is abundant.

Ecclesiastes 8:6

The massive trauma of general war takes many years to clear up, and normalcy is never completely restored by a formal peace. Of all the problems created by modern conflicts, perhaps the most difficult is that of recasting international politics. This perplexity continuously persists because most conflicts that have been fought since the time of Alexander the Great to the present day are classified as politically limited wars. The political aim of the victor was to weaken their enemy. It was not intended to bring a permanent destruction to the conquered group. Due to this designated military confinement, the rival nations of history faced each other in a type of struggle that is presently designated as the "cold war," although such strategies throughout the centuries have been basically comparable.

During World War II, the Communists and democratic factions fought as allies. After the Axis nations were defeated, the United States was undoubtedly the most powerful nation in the world; however, the country was weary of war and regressed from the burden of leadership. In time, the Soviet Union intensified its strength due to its distrust in democracy, thus forcing the countries of lesser authority to choose its mainstay. It led to what was often referred to as the East [Communist bloc] and the West [Free world bloc]. It is believed by most historians that the Cold War between the East and West would continue as long as both Communism and democracy existed. The reality of this political development had its beginning nearly twenty-four centuries ago. In each case it depended upon the positioning of military forces in strategic locations, the integrated maneuvers of a government in every realm of endeavor, or international tensions that were exploited by one party in an effort to manipulate the other.

As we closely examine the book of Daniel to learn additional things that were prophesied to occur in our day, we find Daniel's portrayal of a long, drawn out hostility between opposing political factions referred to as the "king of the north" and the "king of the south." The Scriptures embrace this composite incident from the rule of ancient Greece down to our present day. The prophecy only refers to specific facts of history that would *unquestionably* con-incide with the prophetic description. Intentionally, the prophecy did not declare the name of the two kings since their identity was to vary over the course of centuries.

Chapter Eleven reveals the movements of these two symbolic kings against one another and the affect and influence they have on all mankind. It discloses the philosophy of history, both sacred and profane, revealing to the generations of mankind what was to transpire until the supremacy of God's Kingdom prevails at Armageddon.

Auspicious Beginnings

Darius the Mede, the uncle of Cyrus the Great, was the first ruler of the Medo-Persian Empire. The people of the Medes appear in history first in 836 B.C. and primarily were an Iranian tribe. The origin of the dynasty is quite obscure with the principle source of information originating from the writings of Herodotus. Other than the fact that the Medes became subjugated to the Persians after Cyrus rebelled and usurped the throne from his paramount Astyages, the history of Darius is somewhat indistinct. However, it was during the first year of his reign, or about 536 B.C., that the prophecy was revealed to Daniel and was to span a period in excess of 2,000 years or to the time of the end. The meaning is straight-forward:

> "And as for me, in the first year of Darius the Mede, I stood up to confirm and strengthen him. And now I will show you the truth. Behold, three kings shall arise in Persia; and a fourth shall be far richer than all of them; and when he has become strong through his riches, he shall stir up all against the kingdom of Greece. Then a mighty king shall arise, who shall rule with great dominion and do according to his will" (Daniel 11:1-3).

As previously indicated, the trend of political limited wars were typical in history. There is no assertion made about the end of the Medo-Persian Empire. It simply points to a fourth king that would impose an all-out exertion against Greece.

The three kings of Persia that would assume world rulership or "shall arise" were historically significant. The first was Cyrus the Great who within the short space of twenty years established a vast empire larger than any that had formerly existed. The seizure of the Chaldean capital made this rapid expansion conceivable, and it continued until his death in 529 B.C.

Cambyses, the son of Cyrus, was Cyrus' successor. He conquered Egypt in 525 B.C. and brought all the ancient Near East under one overlord. During the king's absence, a rebellion spread throughout his Asiatic possessions. The chief lord lieutenant of the domain, incited by the priests, organized a movement to gain control of the throne for the Magian pretender named Gaumata. Upon discovering the conditions at home, Cambyses set out from Egypt with his most prepared troops but was murdered on the way. Gaumata was not considered as one of the three kings of prophecy. After nearly eight months, the revolt was crushed by Darius I who killed the usurper and seized the throne for himself.

Darius I became the third predominant king of foresight. He ruled from 521 to 486 B.C. and was constantly occupied in supressing the revolts of subject peoples and improving the administrative structure of the state. He was quite successful in both of these endeavors; however, his ambition for power carried him beyond his tactical ability. He crossed the Hellespont and conquered a large part of the Thacian coast. This maneuver aroused the hostilities of the Athenians, and when he interfered with their trade concernment and tried to collect trade tribute from them, an immediate retaliation ensued. Darius found himself involved in a war with nearly all the states of Greece. After his defeat, he thereafter planned a major revengeful expedition, but he died before he could launch it.

The fourth king was Xerxes I, son of Darius, and he did indeed, "stir up all against the kingdom of Greece." All evidence points to the fact that Xerxes I and King Ahasuerus mentioned in Esther 1:1 are one and the same. His character was marked by unmanly timidity. Xerxes had not inherited his fathers animosity against Greece, but resolved to continue the enterprise to make preparations for the invasion of the oncoming world power. Troops were collected from as many as forty-six countries and according to Herodotus, reached the incredible figure of 5,283,220 fighting men.

In the spring of 480 B.C., Xerxes set out from Sardis with his vast soldiery. Upon arriving at the plain of Doriscus, he found that the enemy land and sea forces only amounted to 2,641,610 fighting men and that the attendants were said to have been greater in number than the warriors. The fear of the Persians was so great that a countless number at once tendered their submission to him. Although Xerxes had twice the strength of the Greeks, it proved to be ineffectual. The army and navy was so large that it was impossible to operate together as a unit. He stationed himself on a high knoll so that he might bestow rewards upon the bravest of his leaders. He witnessed the complete destruction of his navy and fled back to Asia Minor while his army was defeated at Plataea. Strange as it may seem, the invasion had been considered merely as a frontier expedition to the uncivilized confines of the world. Xerxes returned home to rule his empire for the remainder of his life as if nothing had ever transpired. There were seven more Persian kings to rule the empire, and they continued as the fourth world power for approximately 150 years. This does not indicate that the angel erred with reference to the prediction. It only concluded with the fourth king as it was the final intrusive attempt that Persia ever schemed against Greece. As prophetic events throughout the Bible are, in fact, *condensed history,* the remaining kings were passed over to bring to the querier's attention "a mighty king that will rule with great dominion."

In 336 B.C., the Macedonian Alexander the Great commenced his domination. He was crowned by his father Philip II. He was twenty-two years old and did prove to be a "mighty king." By 334 B.C. he was ready to embark upon one of the most brilliant conquests in history. The completeness and the vision with which Alexander carried out his military crusade had lasting effects, even to the import of being consequential to the design of prognosis. However, Alexander's great gratification of world supremacy was to be short-lived. He conquered everything but himself as he became a drunkard and eventually turned into a maniac. God's angel interposes:

> "And when he has arisen, his kingdom shall be broken and divided toward the four winds of heaven, but not to his posterity, nor according to the dominion with which he ruled; for his kingdom shall be plucked up and go to others besides them" (Daniel 11:4).

Steadily, Alexander became uneasy and had hysterics of

remorse at some uncommendable things he may have done. He became ill with malaria, complicated by pneumonia, and by June 28, 323 B.C., the emperor died at thirty-two years old.

Alexander left behind him only one legitimate son named Alexander Allou who was made the partner of Philip Aridaeus, Alexander's half-wit half brother in the empire. His son met a violent death at the hand of one of his father's generals, Cassander and as for Aridaeus, eventually he was murdered by his chief officers near the city of Memphis. Therefore, the empire was not conveyed "to his posterity." Rather, history divided the kingdom toward "the four winds of heaven" with generals Ptolemy Lagus [securing Egypt, Arabia, Libya and Palestine], Seleucus Nicator [receiving eastern Asia, including Babylon, Syria and Persia], Cassander [possessing Macedonia and Greece], and Lysimachus [acquiring Asia Minor and European Thrace]. In time, the male heirs of Cassander died out, and in 285 B.C., Lysimachus assumed the European part of the Empire of Macedonia. Twenty years later, the four states were reduced to two when Seleucus defeated and killed Lysimachus in battle and appropriated his kingdom. The extravaganza of the Kings of Vexation are now disclosed by Daniel:

> "Then the king of the south [south of Daniel's people] shall be strong, but one of his princes shall be stronger than he and his dominion shall be a great dominion" (Daniel 11:5).

The Vexatious Kings

As identified by Daniel, the "king of the south" is one of his [Alexander] "princes" or generals, namely Ptolemy I. In the Macedonian and Greek governors of the Ptolemies, the Egyptians found a government more sensitive and moderate than in their previous self-ruling empire. The rule of the Ptolemies, though an absolute monarchy, was temperate; the rulers considered the interests of the people which in turn increased government revenues and made their power more concrete. It seems, rather, that Egypt conquered the Ptolemies politically than that the Macedonians ruled Egypt. However, Ptolemy I was a man of very extraordinary intellectual gifts who seemed to have done the most to carry out ideas of a systematic organization. The dominant form of government of both the dynasty of the Ptolemies and the Seleucid kings continued to represent them as semi-divine. The Ptolemies signed their decrees "Theos" [God], and the Seleucid monarch adopted the title "Epiphanes," [God manifest].

Among the successors of Alexander, the ablest administrator was Seleucus Nicator. As "king of the north," he established as many as seventy-five colonies in his realm. Among these was Seleucia on the Tigris which contained some 600,000 inhabitants. As a capital for his kingdom, he founded Antioch in Syria, a city that became notable in early Christian history. He attracted colonists from every part of Greece and brought industry and enterprise to every part of the empire. As a promoter of civilization, Seleucus was the most worthy among the successors of Alexander. In time, Seleucus expanded his dominions so that they became greater than those possessed by Ptolemy. The unimaginable predictions are attainable with God. It is especially true as the prophecy continues:

> "After some years they shall make an alliance, and the daughter of the king of the south shall come to the king of the north to make peace; but she shall not retain the strength of her arm, and he and his offspring shall not endure; but she shall be given up, and her attendants, her child, and he who got possession of her" (Daniel 11:6).

Although the king of the north originally ruled over a kingdom far greater than the king of the south, they were at war much of the time with the Ptolemies constantly seeking control of Palestine and Asia Minor.

Ptolemy captured Jerusalem in 312 B.C., and he persuaded the Jews to colonize in Alexandria. The Judean province remained under the control of Ptolemaic Egypt until 198 B.C. Ptolemy I Soter proved to be crafty and prudent and had established a compact and well-ordered realm after fifty years of wars. He died in 283 B.C. at the age of eighty-four and was succeeded by Ptolemy II [Philadelphus] who was of a subtle character and not the Macedonian warrior type.

Seleucus had secured the whole of Alexander's empire except Egypt. In 281 B.C., he left Asia to Antiochus and crossed over to take possession of Macedonia. He reached Chersonese but was assassinated by Ptolemy near Lysimachia. He was succeeded by his son Antiochus I; however, he was killed while attempting to break the growing power of Pergamum. His sudden death prevented him from being recognized by the angel's prophecy to Daniel. His second son Antiochus II assumed the role of the king of the north.

Nations will often band together in a unified action when they are threatened by a common foe or by each other. This is a besetting characteristic that becomes evident throughout the centuries. It will be more conspicuous in the twentieth century when the king of the south and the king of the north are exposed. Keep in mind, as we consider this chapter, that alliances are only veneer in man's determination to rule. World leaders, out of desperation or because of foreseeing some selfish advantage in pursuing such a treaty, will even pledge the life of others to succeed.

The Ptolemaic kingdom extended to Samothrace and encompassed the harbors and coast towns of Cilicia, Trachea, Lycia, Pamphylia and Caria. This was the first of two wars that the king of the south waged against the king of the north. However about 250 B.C., Ptolemy perceived that he was sustaining great losses on the sea margin of Asia Minor, so he made a peace alliance by which Antiochus married his daughter Berenice. Again, the prophecy in part was fulfilled with the "daughter of the king of the south" named.

"The strength of her arm" was her father King Ptolemy II. Therefore, after his death in 246 B.C., her strength was "not retained." Her husband Antiochus II deserted Berenice and her infant son to live again with his former wife Laodice. Laodice, in turn, poisoned him and announced her son Seleucus II, Callinicus king, while her henchmen at Antioch murdered Berenice, her son and attendants thus completing the 309-year-old prediction.

The angel proceeds to foretell a response that would transpire:

> "In those times a branch from her roots shall arise in his place; he shall come against the army and enter the fortress of the king of the north, and he shall deal with them and shall prevail" (Daniel 11:7).

The "roots" specifically refer to her parents Ptolemy II, and his sister-wife Arsinoes. Therefore, the "branch that would arise in his place" could be no other than her brother Ptolemy III who now undertakes the role as king of the south. Without hesitation, he retaliated as one wreaking vengeance and launched his attack against the Seleucid kingdom. Ptolemy marched triumphantly into the heart of the realm of the king of the north as far as Babylonia. His fleets had taken back the seaports his father had lost and subjugated the capital city of Antioch. The zenith of the Ptolemaic power was regained, and he did "prevail."

As we proceed, the prophecy discloses further decadence that was to occur:

> "He shall also carry off to Egypt their gods with their molten images and with their precious vessels of silver and of gold; and for some years he

shall refrain from attacking the king of the north"
(Daniel 11:8).

More than two hundred years previously, or in 525 B.C.,
the Persian King Cambyses made a permanent conquest of
Egypt. In his walkover, he siezed their "molten images" as
well as 2500 "precious vessels of silver and gold." In fulfillment, Ptolemy recovered and deported the ancient Egyptian gods and brought them back to their empery. Due to
internal problems at home, he returned and no longer
engaged actively in war with Seleucus II.
In reprisal, Seleucus II exploited the situation:

"Then the latter shall come into the realm of the
king of the south but shall return into his own
land. His sons shall wage war and assemble a multitude of great forces, which shall come on and
overflow and pass through, and again shall carry
the war as far as his fortress" (Daniel 11:9, 10).

He immediately amassed his troops and struck back in
retribution. He recuperated Northern Syria and several
provinces of Iran; however, he met defeat and retreated to
Antioch. A year later, 227 B.C., Seleucus fell from his horse
and was pronounced dead. He preceded the death of his
humiliator Ptolemy III by six years.
With reference to "his sons" of the same prophecy,
Seleucus was succeeded by his eldest son Seleucus III Soter
who took up the stint of reconquering Asia Minor but met a
violent death by an assassin during encampment. His 18-
year-old brother Antiochus III, [the Great], resumed the role
of king of the north. After making an attempt to reorganize
the kingdom, he assembled a great army machine for an
offense on the king of the south who was now Ptolemy IV.
The military crusade had recovered the central part of Asia
Minor and continued to advance to the outlying provinces
of the north and east. In his avenging spirit of conquest, the
Seleucid arms were almost carried to the boundary of

Egypt, but in 217 B.C., Ptolemy defeated Antiochus and forced him to retreat to his winter quarters at Ptolemais. The king of the south moved militarily:

> "Then the king of the south, moved with anger,
> shall come out and fight with the king of the north;
> and he shall raise a great multitude, but it shall be
> given into his hand. And when the multitude is
> taken, his heart shall be exalted, and he shall cast
> down tens of thousands, but he shall not prevail"
> (Daniel 11:11, 12).

Moving north with nearly 70,000 troops to the city of Raphia, Ptolemy IV met Antiochus and his 60,000 fighting men. The battle was decisive and the Syrian King was "given into his hand." King Ptolemy had slaughtered some 10,000 Syrian troops and 300 horsemen and "taken away" 5,000 more as prisoners. The Egyptian victory where Ptolemy himself was present secured his provinces including Palestine, until the next reign.

Antiochus III, however, did not resign himself to remaining idle after his defeat at Raphia. In his endeavor, he finally came into conflict with the rising power of Rome. The prophecy focuses in on his plan of controlment:

> "For the king of the north shall again raise a multi-
> tude, greater than the former; and after some years
> he shall come on with a great army and abundant
> supplies" (Daniel 11:13).

Rome was now the ruling city of Italy and was responsible for the protection of the Italian coast against invaders. Carthage was the chief offender. Furthermore, there were now certain clashes of interest between Rome and Carthage. The wars by which the Carthaginian power was overthrown are known to history as the Punic Wars. The three wars extended well over a century, but Rome freed Greece from Macedonian control and established itself well as a world power. Rome assumed the responsibility for policing much of the known world but took no territory in foreign realms and announced that all cities were to be free and independent.

Many of the states were dissatisfied and sought aid from Antiochus the Great. Ptolemy IV had died, and his 5-year-old son Ptolemy V became king. Antiochus III and Philip V of Macedonia made an agreement to divide the Ptolemaic holdings. In 198 B.C.,, Palestine was transferred from the Ptolemies to the Seleucids. In 197 B.C., Antiochus moved to Asia Minor to secure coast towns that had recognized Ptolemy as their precursor. The time became difficult for the young king of the south according to Daniel:

> "In those times many shall rise against the king of the south; and the men of violence among your own people shall lift themselves up in order to fulfill the vision; but they shall fail" (Daniel 11:14).

Besides facing the contention from the united kings, the prophecy contends that some of Daniel's people or "men of violence among your own people" were disturbers. In making an effort to run ahead of God or "fulfill the vision," they were sure to "fail." Daniel further discloses:

> "Then the king of the north shall come and throw up siegeworks, and take a well fortified city. And the forces of the south shall not stand, or even his picked troops, for there shall be no strength to stand. But he who comes against him shall do according to his own will, and none shall stand before him; and he shall be in the glorious land, and all of it shall be in his power" (Daniel 11:15, 16).

The "forces of the south" sent by Ptolemy V under General Scopas proved to have "no strength to stand." Antiochus the Great was victorious and drove General Scopas and his "picked troops" back to Sidon, a "fortified city." General Scopas was forced to surrender because of a famine that was expanding by degrees. By bringing Jerusalem under his control, the king of the north stood "in the glorious land." This enterprise brought him into opposition with Rome, and the tension became greater between the powers. Daniel expounds a change of identity:

> "He shall set his face to come with the strength of his whole kingdom, and he shall bring terms of peace and perform them. He shall give him the daughter of women to destroy the kingdom; but it shall not stand or be to his advantage" (Daniel 11:17).

Since the Syrian King had taken away Judea, he was still determined to dominate Egypt "with the strength of his whole kingdom," but unbeknown to Antiochus, the guardians of the young king had turned to Rome and placed Ptolemy under the influence of their combative power. Since his attempts were ineffectual against Rome, Antiochus was reduced to sue for peace on conditions less favorable than he expected. The outlying provinces of the kingdom that he had previously conquered reasserted their independence.

After the peace alliance was formulated, Antiochus gave his own "daughter of women," Cleopatra, to be the young king's wife. In 193 B.C., after Ptolemy was proclaimed of legal age, the marriage was consummated. As her dowry, she was to receive the provinces of Coele-Syria, Phoenicia and Palestine [including the "beauteous land"]. However, since this marriage was a political scheme "to destroy the kingdom" [Egypt], Antiochus had no intention of allowing the provinces to leave his domain. Likewise, according to the prophecy, "it shall not be to his advantage" because Cleopatra sided with her young husband. The angel now discloses the inverted consequences:

> "Afterward he shall turn his face to the coastlands, and shall take many of them; but a commander

shall put an end to his insolence; indeed he shall turn his insolence back upon him. Then he shall turn his face back toward the fortresses of his own land; but he shall stumble and fall, and shall not be found" (Daniel 11:18, 19).

In 192 B.C., Antiochus III tried his strength against the Romans for the coastlands of Asia Minor and Macedonia. He felt that Rome was intruding on his rightful territories in the East. Rome formally declared war on the king of the north, who was stationed at Acarnania. A year later, he passed over into Greece with a totally deficient force and was defeated by the Romans at Thermopylae. In 189 B.C., a final peace arrangement was made, but Antiochus III again attempted a fresh expedition to the east and expired in Luristan "not to be found" in history thereafter.

His son Seleucus IV Philopator reigned for about nine years and suffered financial difficulties due to his father's great war losses and the indemnity that he was required to pay Rome. He was assassinated by his minister Heliodorus who fruitlessly aspired after the throne for himself. Since the rightful heir Demetrius, son of Seleucus, was retained in Rome as a hostage since childhood, the brother of Seleucus, Antiochus IV, was placed upon the throne. However, eventually he was also taken to Rome and held hostage for nearly fourteen years. Though friendly to Rome, he was prevented from successfully concluding his war against Egypt. After leaving Rome, he resided in Athens. He had brought to his kingdom an admiration for his passion for Hellenic culture.

In an effort to exalt himself as "God Manifest," [the meaning of his adopted surname, Epiphanes], Antiochus made an effort to grecize Judea and Jerusalem. He installed the high priest of his choice in the temple and tried to suppress the practices of Judaism by force. This provoked the insurrection of the Jews under Judah Maccabeus in 167 B.C. After Judah led them to a series of victories against a much larger force, they attained religious freedom in 164 B.C. and established political independence by 142 B.C. Antiochus IV died in 163 B.C., leaving his younger son Antiochus V Eupater as king of the north.

Ptolemy V tried to retrieve the provinces that should have come to him as Cleopatra's dowry, but in his endeavor, he was poisoned by an unknown assailant. His infant son Ptolemy VI Philometor assumed the role of king of the south under the regency of his mother Cleopatra. The role was to remain with Egypt for many centuries to come. In a well-known event of history, Egypt's Queen Cleopatra VII sought to restore the power of the Ptolemaic Empire to what it was previously by winning to her support Caesar and later Anthony. Upon Anthony's suicide after the decisive battle of Actium in 31 B.C., she sought to excite the young Octavian but failed and committed suicide rather than dignify his victory.

After Antiochus V, there were sixteen more independent kings of the Seleucid dynasty before the last one was dethroned in 65 B.C. by Roman General Pompey the Great. *Rome definitely took up the role of the king of the north.* In 63 B.C., Jerusalem fell before the prophetic king with the Egyptian king unable to discourage it.

In the struggle for power, Octavian triumphs and becomes the absolute ruler of Rome. It was decreed by the Senate that he should add to his name the honorary title *Augustus,* meaning "majestic" (compare Acts 25:21, 25). Though the Senate and Assembly were continued, a monarchy had really been established, for it was within his power to name his own successor and to appoint the senators. He was also granted the right to command the army, and this gave him the power to decide on peace or war. God's angel continues to foresee the contention between the north and the south:

"Then shall arise in his place one who shall send
an exactor of the tribute through the glory of the

kingdom; but within a few days he shall be broken, neither in anger nor in battle" (Daniel 11:20).

In the year 2 B.C., the "exactor" took place. The Christian writer Luke develops the incident when he speaks of "those days when a decree went out from Caesar Augustus that all the world should be enrolled. [This was the first enrollment since Quirinius was governor of Syria]. And all went to be enrolled, each to his own city" (Luke 2:1-3). This registration was not merely for the purpose of recording world population but more importantly, for the purpose of taxation and the induction of men into military service. The angel also included the circumstances in revelation to Daniel because the "exactor" was instrumental in maneuvering Joseph and his wife Mary to Bethlehem so Jesus could be born there, thus fulfilling the prophecy of Micah (Micah 5:2).

Emperor Augustus established the Praetorian Guards and made them a standing army for the personal protection of the Roman emperors. They were divided into three cohorts, each consisting of a thousand men. The guard continued until 312 A.D. when it was abolished by Emperor Constantine. Augustus died on August 19, A.D. 14, after a glorious and successful reign, and he was numbered among the gods.

The prophecy now discloses the successor of Augustus and one that would have a cognizable rapport with the earthly life of the Son of God:

"In his place shall arise a contemptible person to whom royal majesty had not been given; he shall come in without warning and obtain the kingdom by flatteries. Armies shall be utterly swept away before him and broken, and the prince of the covenant also" (Daniel 11:21, 22).

Augustus had, throughout his reign, sought to procure a successor to insure the perpetuation of the empery. In this undertaking, he tried to combine inheritance, either by blood, marriage or adoption, with the selection of the best available person. Each one of the possible candidates had predeceased him leaving only one choice. The "contemptible person" proved to be Tiberius Caesar, the stepson of the emperor. Augustus despised this stepson because of his questionable nature, and history did indicate him to be an unpopular ruler. Daniel's prediction was true, as the "royal majesty" was only the choice of elimination.

With reference to the "flatteries," *The Encyclopaedia Britannica* characterizes his artfulness when they say that "historians of Rome in ancient times remembered Tiberius chiefly as the sovereign under whose rule prosecution for treason on slight pretexts first became rife, and the hateful body of informers was first allowed to fatten on the gain of judicial murder. . . ." But the history of the state trials of Tiberius' reign shows conclusively that the straining of the law proceeded in the first instance from the eager *flattery* of the senate. . . .

Before Tiberius ascended to the throne, Germanicus, the son of Tiberius' brother Drusus and the one whom Augustus had influenced Tiberius to adopt as a possible successor, was commander of the Roman soldiery on the Rhine River. He was victorious in suppressing the German revolt and campaigned in Germany with stinted success. He defeated Arminius, whose kingdom then broke up, and redeemed the eagle of Varus' legions. In this way, "armies were utterly swept away" and were "broken." The prophecy further speaks of the "prince of the covenant," and according to the law of *laesa majestas*, the Son of God was handed over to the masses to be "broken" or crucified (John 19:12-16).

Making further attributions to Tiberius, the angel said to Daniel:

"And from the time that an alliance is made with

124

him he shall act deceitfully, and he shall become strong with a small nation" (Daniel 11:23).

Unlike Augustus Caesar who was considered *princeps* or "first citizen" and maintained his rule as a monarch, Tiberius was enleagued constitutionally and depended upon the Senate. However, history reveals that deceitfully he became reliant upon the "small nation" in lieu of the Senate or Assembly. The small nation was undeniably the "Praetorian Guard" which, like a bodyguard, surrounded the person of the emperor. The concentration of this force was on the eastern edge of the city of Rome in fortified barracks. Under the advice of Sejanus, the commander of the Guard, they were later encamped in Rome and were frequently divided between two incumbents. They became so powerful that they could overthrow emperors whenever they chose. By means of the "small nation," Tiberius remained "strong."

> "Without warning he shall come into the richest parts of the province; and he shall do what neither his fathers nor his fathers' fathers have done, scattering among them plunder, spoil and goods. He shall devise plans against strongholds, but only for a time" (Daniel 11:24).

Few emperors have ever possessed such mental vision for the great care of the Roman provinces. Many historians have questioned whether he ever liked or was liked by anyone, but when it came to duty, he was quite thorough, although in an unlovable mode. Tiberius was capable in every department of the state, especially when it involved taxation and the economy. When economic conditions were depressed in neighboring countries, Tiberius always was able to demonstrate generosity. Throughout his reign, his guiding principles were maintained with an almost superstitious reverence. After his death in A.D. 37, he left all people that were subjugated to the empire in a posture of comfort and prosperity that "neither his fathers nor his fathers' fathers have ever done."

Caligula was of unsound mind who, among other whimsies, made his horse a consul. His own officers, led by Cassius Chaerea, finally assassinated him. The Praetorian Guard forced the Senate to select Claudius, the younger brother of Germanicus, as emperor.

While Christ and his disciples were preaching the Gospel of the Kingdom of God and a love that yields temperance toward materialistic gain, the Italians, as far removed as possible from that of the Galilean, were forging into new markets, unfolding new enterprises, exploring new lands and crying out for new conquests. Claudius, the cloddish, self-indulgent imbecile, began the serious conquest of Britain and added Mauretania, Thrace and Judea to the Roman provinces. The activities of the king of the north are pre-examined further:

> "And he shall stir up his power and his courage against the king of the south with a great army; and the king of the south shall wage war with an exceedingly great and mighty army; but he shall not stand, for plots shall be devised against him. Even those who eat his rich food shall be his undoing; his army shall be swept away, and many shall fall down slain" (Daniel 11:25, 26).

This verse introduces Emperor Aurelian as the king of the north. During the third century, hidden troubles erupted into violent storms. Externally, the frontier broke open under the attacks of Sassanid Persia to the east and the Germanic tribes to the north. The most dangerous threat, however, came from the king of the south Queen Zenobia of Palmyra. She seized control of the eastern provinces for a few years around 270 A.D. Her husband King Odaenathus was the headmost commander of the East. About 267 A.D., he and his sons were assassinated, supposedly by a vengeful nephew. His wife Zenobia took over their positions and planned to make Palmyra the dominant city of the Roman Empire in the east. She strengthened and adorned it to such an extent that it ranked with the large cities of the Roman world.

Aurelian, as king of the north, sensed that the ambitious policy established by Queen Zenobia had become a threat to the unity of the Roman empery. In 272 A.D., Aurelian revived vigor enough in the Roman armies to vanquish her or "the army was swept away." He took her to Rome where she lived quietly until the end of her days. Even to this day, although there are pronounced ruins that signify a vast city once existed, the population of Palmyra was reduced to that of a village.

The re-establishment of the oneness of the empire was complete. The Senate conveyed upon him the deserved title of "Restorer," and he was the first Roman emperor to wear the diadem, whereas he was entitled Lord and God. In 274 A.D., he started on an expedition against Persia. While on the march between Heracleia and Byzantium, he was assassinated by a conspiracy maneuvered by his secretary Eros. According to the prophetic word, "those who eat his rich food shall be his undoing."

After the reign of Aurelian, jealousies, quarrels and civil wars were soon agonizing the empire again but under conditions that had never occurred before. In time, the sovereignty of the empire was divided between two emperors. They were Constantine, son of Constantius who reigned in the west and one Licinius, whose dominion was in the east. Under these conditions, the king of the north became indistinct and will remain aloof until the predicted event becomes right (Compare Proverbs 4:18). Germanic barbarians on the northern frontiers of the empire proceeded to launch out against many of the provinces, and in several regions, they made permanent victories. To the north of the Balkan Peninsula, the Goths were prepared to take advantage of any further impotency exhibited by the

Roman Empire. Relations between the two emperors were interrupted by Licinius' anti-Christian policy and finally erupted into war. He was defeated by Constantine's son Chrispus at Adrianople and again at Chrysopolis in Anatolia. He then surrendered and was executed one year later.

Constantine reunited the empire and became sole ruler of Rome. In the final stages, the contest had become somewhat refracted. Rather than political, it was a trial of strength between expiring paganism in the Roman world and *militant* Christianity. The crafty Constantine saw the political significance to which the popular form of Christianity had risen, and he identified himself with it by a conversion which undeservedly glorified his own name. The alleged conversion became an important event in history. The state became a sort of church and the church a sort of state. The emperor preached and convoked councils, and the bishops had become state officials who traveled by the imperial courier service to various provinces of the empire.

Another event marked in history was the reconstruction of the magnificent Greek city of Byzantium. Constantine conveyed his imperial residence there and raised it to an unrealistic equality with Rome. The old Rome dwindled in rank and prestige from that day, and the new Rome became the city of Constantine, or Constantinople.

The last independent emperor to rule was Theodosius. The empire for the last time was united under one lord. At the beginning of the year 395, Theodosius died, and his two weak sons Arcadius and Honorius divided the perishing empire between themselves. Honorius, a child of eleven, received the western section, and Arcadius, at the age of eighteen, took the eastern section with its capital at Constantinople. Egypt fell to Arcadius and became a province of the eastern division of the empire.

The bishop of Rome was decreed by emperor Valentinian III to have all authority and took precedence over all the other bishops. Therefore, "Papa" or pope came to be applied to Leo I with the bishopric of Rome referred to as the "Holy See." The western Church had broken entirely with the eastern, and the eastern emperor at Constantinople was a female usurper by the name of Irene. However, on Christmas day in the year 800, Pope Leo III took it upon himself to crown the Frankish King Charlemagne emperor of the Western Roman Empire. Since both empires were claiming to be Christian, Charlemagne added a second head to the eagle in his insignia to indicate that the Empires of Rome and Germany were united.

In 962 A.D., Otho I [the Great] became king of the Saxon dynasty. He was crowned by Pope John XII in Rome, and his kingdom became known as the *Holy Roman Empire of the German Nation*. However, Germany proved to be the superior power after the Holy Roman Empire came to an infamous end subjugated by the French emperor Napoleon Bonaparte. This was after 1,006 years, thus discrediting their claim that it was the millennial kingdom of God. In 1870, Italy was established as an entity independent of the Roman popes of the Vatican.

Although outwardly the Court of Napoleon was still fulgurating and lavish as ever, the Emperor was no longer capable of firm decisions. In 1870, a Spanish revolution broke out and swept away Napoleon, Olivier, and the Liberal Empire and at the same time enabled the dream of Germany to become an established fact.

The moment had now come when it would be possible to establish a strong centralized state in Germany. On December 2, 1870, King Ludwig of Bavaria addressed a letter to King William of Prussia [drafted by Bismarck] inviting him to assume the imperial title. On January 18, 1871, William I was declared Caesar or Kaiser, thus, the king of the north made his appearance and identified himself publicly. As governments evolve toward the time of the end and international power struggles between two geopolitical ideas emerge, the kings of vexation once again re-enact their roles according to God's appointed time.

Great Britain became the seventh world power of Bible

prophecy during the seventeenth century. With the Monroe Doctrine enunciated in 1823, it was only reasonable to conclude that a coalition would be formed thus establishing the Anglo-American dual world power. During the war with Napoleon Bonaparte, the British drove the French out of Egypt, and in 1914, Egypt became a British Protectorate. It has now become evident that the opponent of the new Germanic Confederation proves to be the democratic British and American powers as they assume the role of king of the south.

The starting point of Daniel's prophecy was in ancient time, but its description of the surging vexation of such opposing forces extends all the way down through history to our time. The scene presented at the close of the prophecy will reveal two dominant entities especially as they become manifest as a result of the Great War of 1914. Two political ideologies are represented by them, and each bloc fears an expansion by violent aggression on the part of the other. God's angel opens the threshold to the twentieth century:

> "And as for the two kings, their minds shall be bent on mischief; they shall speak lies at the same table, but to no avail; for the end is yet to be at the time appointed" (Daniel 11:27).

The Anglo-American accord had an increasing importance with the passing years. It did not mean the complete dispersion of former competition. Rather, the incessant threat to both nations of the imperialistic ambitions of Germany continued to pull them together. As far as America's participation in world affairs went, they continued refusal to make any commitments that infringed upon the nation's freedoms. This policy continued until America was drawn into the world conflict of 1914 although they had taken part in the international peace conferences that were held at The Hague in 1899 and 1907.

The king of the north and the king of the south have

continually seated themselves "at the same table" with "their minds bent on mischief." Each claimed to rule by the sanctification of God and have used this credence to justify their endeavors. Constant friction between the two kings and being within their own camp of nations forced each to embark upon the policy of alliances.

There were some seventy-two alliances, treaties or pacts that were negotiated from the time Germany declared her supremacy to the outbreak of World War I. The two most predominant of the system of alliances were the *Triple Alliance* which consisted of Germany, Austria and Italy. They entered into this principle of "reciprocal compensations" and the *Triple Entente*, which was a coalition of France, Russia and England. In this manner, the Triple Entente was to checkmate the Triple Alliance, and the balance of power was thus unreliably maintained. However, this process of lying and deceitful conduct did not assure either king of a peaceful world. More is aforesaid to Daniel with the king of the north in mind:

> "And he shall return to his land with great substance, but his heart shall be set against the holy covenant. And he shall work his will, and return to his own land" (Daniel 11:28).

The long and extraordinary reign of the emperor William I was ended by his death in 1888. His son Frederick III was dying from an incurable disease and survived his father by only three months. The son of Frederick, William II [Kaiser Wilhelm], ascended to the throne at age twenty-nine. Upon his "return home" to the ancient condition of the king of the north, he proceeded to build up an absolutist monarchial form of rule. He never doubted that the monarchy was a divine institution and that God had set him in his place. Through this endeavor, "great substance" resulted as he set about enlarging his military forces. This would increase needed prestige and ensure the empire's share in the apportionment of the world's territories. "His heart was set against the holy covenant" in that he relied upon his own materialistic inclination rather than the Kingdom covenant by Christ. History will reveal that neither of the two kings have ever "sought first the Kingdom," but in a wholehearted fashion, the two kings assumed that their will was that of God.

As world domination became the fervent question, and with so much combustible hatred stored up, only a spark was needed to touch off the greatest war in history up to that time. The angel continues:

> "At the time appointed [1914], he shall return and
> come into the south; but it shall not be this time as
> it was before" (Daniel 11:29).

On August 1, 1914, Germany declared war on Russia. The British cabinet voted to give France assurances to protect the coast against German attack. Two days later, Germany declares war on France due to the conviction that France would come to Russia's support. On the fourth day of August, the king of the south [through Great Britain] invaded Belgium and made a declaration of war against Germany [the king of the north].

The military status was "not as it was before" when the king was the Roman Empire. The king of the north during the twentieth century was confronting the king of the south who was already holding the position of the seventh world power. Speaking further on the dissimilarity with former times, the angel continues:

> "For ships of Kittim shall come against him, and
> he shall be afraid and withdraw, and shall turn
> back and be enraged and take action against the
> holy covenant. He shall turn back and give heed to
> those who forsake the holy covenant" (Daniel
> 11:30).

The German admiralty realized the transcendence of the "ships of Kittim" [British navy] and therefore ordered its navy stationed and protected in the Kiel harbor. The British fleet eliminated the German merchant and naval fleet from the high seas, especially after the German submarine U-20 sank the British liner Lusitania. On April 6, 1917, the United States declared war on Germany, thus bringing together the Anglo-American dual world power against the rival king. The king of the north became "afraid and withdrew" as the Armistice was signed on November 11, 1918.

For twenty-eight years, the impulsive Kaiser seized the helm of the ship of state and found himself in control of the second most powerful military machine in the world. The autocrat had been "against the holy covenant" by his independently becoming a vital and disquieting force in European society. It's ironic that this seemingly supreme war lord was exiled until his death on June 4, 1941. Under these conditions, how is it possible for the king of the north to be "enraged and take action against the holy covenant?"

The "enraged one" that turned back proved to be Adolph Hitler. The life of the Hitler cabinet depended upon the alliance of the Nazi and the Nationalists. Since the two parties were equally victorious in the elections, Hitler proceeded to crush all opposition and set up the Third Reich. To effect the totalitarized state, the Nazis took several steps with regard to religion. Among those were the submission of the new unified German Evangelical Church, headed by the Lutheran Friedrich von Bodelschwingh. Although pastor Martin Niemeller objected, he eventually pledged his loyalty. In 1933, Hitler and Pope Pius XI reached a concordant guaranteeing freedom of worship. In turn, the Church agreed to dissolve the Catholic Center Party and pledge their support to the Third Reich. Millions of Catholics, both clerical and lay, upheld the regime wholeheartedly, persecution of the Jews and all. It is this act of swearing an oath to a demonic plan by those who profess Christianity that creates "action against the holy covenant."

The angel now indicates a complete change of character:

> "Forces from him shall appear and profane the temple and fortress, and shall take away the continued burnt offering. And they shall set up the abomination that makes desolate" (Daniel 11:31).

"Forces from him" primarily denotes the armed forces that upheld the king of the north during the conflict against the king of the south. Before, during, and after World War II, changes had developed that altered the course of the human race dramatically.

By the end of July 1917, the Russian front had corroded before the enemy. The king of the north had already assisted world communism when the obscure exile had returned to Russia under the protection of Kaiser Wilhelm. Ulianoff, who called himself Lenin, seized the control of power and organized the Russian Revolution. The instruments of his strength were a highly organized Communist Party, a secret police and the Red Army. In October 1934, Soviet Russia was admitted to membership in the League of Nations.

In August of 1939, Great Britain and France were mediating with Russia when suddenly they displaced their allegiance to Nazi Germany. They completed a seven-year trade agreement and unexpectedly, a ten-year nonaggression pact. The Russians made this about-face because they were precluded from the negotiations over the Czechoslovakian crisis and blamed the British and the French. Hitler's reason was the obsessive fear of a war on two fronts, a war against the powers to the east and to the west. He was able to arrange a division of Poland with Stalin, thus eliminating Russian intervention from the west.

After nearly two years of being leagued with Russia, Hitler's cunning ambition surfaced as the German armies invaded their co-partner. It forced Russia onto the side of the democratic king of the south, where Great Britain concluded a mutual-aid treaty on July 13, 1941. They assisted in the defeat of the Nazi regime and with crafty strategy took over the position of the dictatorial king of the north, thus creating a new rivalry between the two kings of vexation. The events that impetuously followed revealed the Communist power and their objection of world domination.

As a nation where fear and skepticism are characteristic, it was not unusual that Russia should feel the need for observant or friendly nations on her borders and be resolved to keep such nations under its influence, if not direct control. It created a pursuit for power and a struggle between opposing ideologies such as never existed before. As both Soviet and American policy continued to electrify, the enmeshments of what was becoming the "cold war" could no longer be ignored. Being a godless society has caused the king of the north to "take away the continual burnt offering" as well as banning the spread of the Kingdom truth by those who identified themselves as not possessing the mark of the beast [Revelation 13:16-18].

What is the "abomination that makes desolate?" [Compare Matthew 24:15]. As revealed in the chapter Seven Heads of Predominance, it was the abominable counterfeit for God's Kingdom, the image of the wild beast, that the League of Nations which was eventually crowned as the United Nations, the image for international worship.

If the king of the north cannot destroy by persecution or fear tactics, he will endear with flattery:

> "He shall seduce with flattery those who violate the covenant; but the people who know their God shall stand firm and take action. And those among the people who are wise shall make many understand, though they shall fall by sword and flame, by captivity and plunder, for some days" (Daniel 11:32, 33).

The king of the north, whether Nazi or Communist, makes

an effort to persuade religious bodies that his totalitarian policies are not much different from those of militant Christendom. He must dominate the religious systems in order to maintain the logic of his professed atheism. With religious backing, to a degree, the king of the north's position is strengthened before common people. Under the tsars, the Orthodox Church was the established church, and the majority of people were associated. Other religions, to some measure, were recognized but did not enjoy the same freedoms. Rather than have a religious system with international connections, they prefer an independent national religious system. However, "with flattery" or smooth talk, they have made concessions to the major denominations, although their activities continue to be somewhat circumscribed. Those who take an uncompromising stand for God's Kingdom and acquire spiritual wisdom that is generated through the Scriptures "shall stand firm and take action." The angel further emphasizes the realization that only a few will shun seduction and allow refinement to renew their mind [Compare Matthew 7:13, 14], but many will continue to apostatize and sell themselves as hired prostitutes:

> "When they fall, they shall receive a little help. And many shall join themselves to them with flattery; and some of those who are wise shall fall, to refine and to cleanse them and to make them white, until the time of the end, for it is yet for the time appointed" (Daniel 11:34, 35).

This is understood to a greater extent when one views the fiery trials of persecution as a test of our willingness to serve the Creator amid arduous opposition.

God's angel now gives us a true characterization of the modern day king of the north. This should establish the accuracy of history foretold in advance:

> "And the king shall do according to his will; he

will exalt himself and magnify himself above every god, and shall speak astonishing things against the God of gods. He shall prosper till the indignation is accomplished; for what is determined shall be done. He shall give no heed to the gods of his fathers, or to the one beloved by women; he shall not give heed to any other god, for he shall magnify himself above all. He shall honor the god of fortresses instead of these; a god whom his fathers did not know he shall honor with gold and silver, with precious stones and costly gifts" (Daniel 11:36-38).

As the ancient counterpart of the king of the north accepted the title of god, the modern successor assumes the role convincingly. In his own mind, he has "magnified himself" over every other man-made god that ever existed since the beginning of the march of world powers, as well as the "God of gods." The "women" [weaker vessels] denote agents or nations that are subservient to the king and his disregard for their gods. He requires all subjects to worship the state, as all subjects are considered inferior to him.

In addition to elevating himself above the creation of God, the king of the north attributes "honor to the god of fortresses." Since World War II, Russia has accumulated the largest armed forces in the world with an estimated total of 4 million persons. On August 27, 1957, they tested their first intercontinental ballistic missile, over a year before the United States. Two months later, continuing to embarrass the king of the south, they launched the first satellite into space [Sputnik No. 1]. On November 3, the second Sputnik, carrying a dog as passenger, was rocketed into orbit.

The king of the south accuses the Communist rival king of obstructing all endeavors to secure international peace. The need for disarmament agreements became more critical from 1950 on. One Polaris submarine with its missiles and nuclear warheads contains more destructive power than all of the weapons used in World War II. Even if a nation should attack another with nuclear weapons, it would in all probability be destroyed by a counter-attack. Additionally, the high cost of countries entering into the nuclear armaments race is astronomical. There is a history of disarmament agreements and equally a history of breaking the commitment as the minds of heads of state continue to be "bent on mischief and speak lies at the same table."

The territorial expansion of the northern king is the topic of further consideration:

> "He shall deal with the strongest fortresses by the help of a foreign god; those who acknowledge him he shall magnify with honor. He shall divide the land for a price" (Daniel 11:39).

The Nazi aggression would magnify the defeated nation "with honor" if the king of the north was acknowledged as supreme. For a proper price, it would result in dividing out territories for rulership or acquiring prestige. When Hitler invaded Austria in 1938, Cardinal Theodore Innitzer of Vienna wrote him and closed the letter with "Heil Hitler." Historians remember that when the Catholic bishops held their Fulda Conference of 1940, a unanimous decision was reached to pledge their allegiance to the Third Reich.

After 1945, the Communist king of the north committed aggressions with his foreign "god of fortresses." The United States did not want to see Germany become the pawn in an East-West struggle, but it was prepared to fulfill its responsibilities as an occupying power for as long as necessary. In February 1948 the United States, Great Britain and France merged their zones and set up a joint administration in West Germany. The Soviets retorted by tightening their hold on East Germany and attempted to drive the western allies out of Berlin. In June of that year, the Soviets established a blockade which still defaces the landscape today.

The satellites of the king of the north were intervening more and more directly in the internal affairs of insolvent countries. Eventually, Russia had taken over the Baltic

states of Latvia, Estonia and Lithuania. In 1946, they organized Communist governments in Bulgaria and Romania.
In 1947, Hungary and Poland joined this quest for universal
supremacy, and the following year, the king of the north
seized full power in Czechoslovakia. Yugoslavia, Albania,
Enver and Hoxha had already established a Communist
government as the Iron Curtain continues to descend.

By the close of 1949, the forces under Chiang Kai-shek
were driven from the mainland to take refuge in Formosa.
By this time, it was abundantly clear that Soviet Russia was
actively supporting Communist China. This incipient civil
war only intensified the situation in Korea where separate
zones of Russian and American occupation were divided
by the 38th parallel. Hostilities were precipitated when the
North Koreans suddenly drove across the established de-
marcation. Behind them were the masters of the Kremlin
who were playing fervently their role as the rival king.

The king of the south had been determined to maintain
his status as the world's foregoer. Although his efforts have
been substantial, it has not prevented the king of the north
from becoming equally strong with the realization that
nuclear space-age warfare would be suicidal. This situation
is clearly expounded to Daniel by the angel:

> "At the time of the end, the king of the south shall
> attack him; but the king of the north shall rush
> upon him like a whirlwind, with many ships; and
> he shall come into countries and shall overflow
> and pass through" (Daniel 11:40).

This quotation included new challenges that plagued both
kings in their vexation for power: the missile gap that created Russian superiority—the U-2 incident—the Bay of Pigs
where the United States lost face—the continuation of the
space race—the Cuban missile crisis—the invasion of
Czechoslovakia in 1968— Communist aggression in Latin
America—the Vietnam War—the invasion of Afghanistan.

The prophecy now discloses what will transpire in the near future or just before Armageddon:

"He shall come into the glorious land and tens of thousands shall fall, but these shall be delivered out of his hand: Edom and Moab and the main part of the Ammonites. He shall stretch out his hand against the countries, and the land of Egypt shall not escape. He shall become ruler of the treasures of gold and silver, and all the precious things of Egypt; and the Libyans and the Ethiopians shall follow in his train" (Daniel 11:41-43).

Earlier in this chapter, the "glorious land" [verse 16] referred to the literal land of Judah. It was prophesied that the person of the king of the north, Antiochus III, would "stand in the glorious land." The Scriptures irrefutably signify that literal Israel, *as a nation*, was no longer considered to have "chosen people" after 70 A.D. The Scriptures refer to Israelis in a spiritual sense, or as those true Christians that are not a part of organized religion or their political paramours, and who make up a minority in comparison to those who practice a counterfeit Christianity. The identifying element of the two distinguished classes will come to light in the chapter "The Great Harlot."

Since the "glorious land" is viewed from a spiritual standpoint, one would have to present the rest of the prophecy in the same sense. "Edom and Moab and the main part of the Ammonites" in ancient times bordered the land of Judah and were persistent enemies of God's people. True Christians are active throughout the world in their proclamation of God's Kingdom, therefore, the named districts would picture the case-hardened opponents of Christianity whether nation or organizations. Naturally, as allies of the king of the north, they would be "delivered out of his hand."

Egypt, likewise, must be viewed spiritually since the prophecy today could not have direct reference to the one location. The Communist king of the north claims the whole world as his objective and strives to accomplish this without the employment of general war. He continues to "stretch out his hand against the countries and the land of Egypt" [the world]. Egypt has to be thus observed, with all reasonableness, the same as Revelation 11:8 where it speaks of the two witnesses that were killed and remained on the streets—it relates, "and Egypt where their Lord was crucified." It was not literal Egypt that was responsible for Christ's death, but the entire known world. How far the line of the north's "stretching hand" will reach before the time of the end is unpredictable. The composite signs as correlated in the chapter, "Stump For Seven Times" proves beyond a doubt that, in all probability, *the end of civilization as we know it will culminate before the end of this century.* It is foretold that the king of the north will gain control over the "treasures of gold and silver," including "the precious things" [oil]. Those who are neighbors to this world [Libya and Ethiopia were neighbors to literal Egypt] will "follow his train." It will mean a sizable loss to the king of the south in many ways.

The angel finally sheds light on the dominant question that torments the populus to no end. Is a nuclear holocaust inevitable?

> "But tidings [reports] from the east and the north shall alarm him, and he shall go forth with great fury to exterminate and utterly destroy many. And he shall pitch his palatial tents between the sea and the glorious holy mountain; yet he shall come to his end, with none to help him" (Daniel 11:44, 45).

The critical premise to understanding this text is determined by discovering the location of the king of the north. The prophecy indicated that the king had pushed south and entered into the land of Egypt. From this location, the glorious land, or Judah, was literally to his north and east, or northeast. Therefore, the "reports" come from God's servants in this time of the end that disturb the king. Verse 32 asserted that the people who know their God shall . . . "take action" or proclaim vengeance against the king. Then again, the truth really stems from God and his Son, Christ Jesus. Scripturally, they are located in the north [Psalms 48:2] and from the rising of the sun, or east [Revelation 16:12].

To reiterate Daniel's point of view, his tents are between the sea [Mediterranean Sea] and the glorious holy mountain [Mount Zion]. Therefore, spiritually it is the attack on God's servants that shorten the days for the sake of the elect [Compare Matthew 24:22] and bring about his downfall.

The prophecy assures us emphatically that the end of the king of the north and the king of the south will not be determined by either crowned head. In light of Revelation 11:18, *there will be no nuclear catastrophe* because God himself will "destroy the destroyers of the earth."

Conclusively, within each nation there grew up by degrees an impudent system of justice, but between nations there was never a common ground for laws. Religion made an effort to compensate for the blundering attempts of man ruling man, but even that agency was reduced to denominational separatism with no foreseeable means of healing the breach. While the swiftly gathering clouds of external pressures envelop the nation, only a total annihilation of these systems would usher in lasting peace in a righteous new order. The Scriptures indicate that such events are soon to take place, and nothing can prevent the final consummation.

Chapter 7
Stump for Seven Times

> . . . I will blow upon you with the fire
> of my wrath; and I will deliver you
> into the hands of brutal man, skillful
> to destroy.

Ezekiel 21:31

The technical conditioning of a war machine has no counterpart in the psychological edification of the public mind. Nothing was nearer to the thoughts of the average civilian than the summer holiday and nothing more remote than the prospect of a world war. Of all emotions of the heart, the most perilous is international hatred. The German government, which might have prevented the war, took the responsibility of declaring it. None of the governing factors of the war had been foreseen. Nobody anticipated that nearly all the world would be drawn in, or that it would be a war of peoples waged to the point of extermination. On July 30, 1914, the first of a series of war declarations was pronounced. Twenty-three nations became involved in a new era of devastating world conflict, World War I.

Another ruinous blow of equal importance was enacted over six hundred years before our common era. Prophetically, it was a time in history that would have a direct bearing on the Great War. It befell the wifely nation of Israel whose moral debasement and national degradation became detestable to her heavenly husband.

The Alienated Kingdom

King Solomon had none of the military energy of David, his father. He unnerved his rule to the extent that a large part of David's conquests was lost. His policy was one of peace, and it might have given joy to his people if his unyielding extravagance had not consumed its productive harvest. At Solomon's death, an outburst of rebellion re-opened the old division between the tribes of Judah and Benjamin on one side and the remaining ten tribes on the other. Hereafter, there were two Hebrew kingdoms— Israel and Judah—the latter maintaining Jerusalem for its capital and upholding David's royal house. Solomon's son Rehoboam was the first of its kings. Israel crowned Jeroboam.

The southern kingdom was small and impotent, and although it had David's capital and Solomon's temple, it dropped to a lower historical rank. Rehoboam retained the throne, and his descendants reigned in long succession. Stability of government was a blessing not shared by the rival kingdom in the north.

Unlike the Kingdom of Judah, Israel had three radical dynasty changes to occur within forty years. The last of these gave Israel a strong ruler in Omri, the general of its army who established a stronger basis of government and who founded the city of Samaria to be its capital. Omri's son Ahab had the wisdom to make peace with Judah, but his marriage to Jezebel had depressive results. Under her influence, he imported the worship of the Tyrian Baalm. He built a temple in Samaria and instated to the country a great number of priests of the idolatrous cult. Likewise in Judah, Rehoboam "did what is displeasing to Yahweh, arousing his resentment more than his ancestors did by the sins they committed, they who had built themselves high places, and had set up pillars and sacred poles on every hill" (I Kings 14:22, 23).

But now there came forth in Israel a dauntless voice of denunciation. It was that of the prophet Elijah who seems to have stood nearly alone at the beginning in defiant opposition to the king and queen. However, Elijah and Elisha, his disciple, were victorious in bringing an end to the priests of

144

Baal and suppressing idolatrous worship. Two sons of Ahab reigned after him. Their mother was still living and exercised an influence that was bane in many ways. Then a bloody revolution exterminated the family of Ahab and raised Jehu, the commander of the troops, to the throne. Baal was overthrown, and Israel returned to the worship of the one true God. Eventually, Jehu himself fell into idolatrous practices. Military violence from the second world power of Assyria broke off the hereditary succession after the obscure and probably agonizing reign of Zachariah.

Meanwhile, the kingdom of Judah had been rising to more importance and exhibiting more strength than at any former time in history, but her condemnation was already at the door. Jeremiah began his prophecy in the thirteenth year of Josiah's reign, about seventy years after Isaiah's death, and continued to do so through the troubled times of the Babylonian invasions. His utterances were regarded as an evil omen by the rulers of Jerusalem, and he was subjected to cruel persecution. Unlike Ezekiel who prophesied from Babylon, Jeremiah saw the city besieged and taken, his warnings neglected but fulfilled and saw Jerusalem become a heap of ruins. He foretold the precise date of the Captivity, the fate of King Zedekiah, the return of the Jews and the fall of many nations.

In the fourth year of the reign of King Jehoiakim of Judah, Nebuchadnezzar became king of Babylon. Jeremiah spoke of the executional work he would perform in desolating Jerusalem:

> "The word that came to Jeremiah concerning all the people of Judah. . . . For twenty-three years, the word of the Lord has come to me, and I have spoken persistently to you, but you have not listened. . . . Therefore thus says the Lord of hosts: Because you have not obeyed my words, behold I will send for all the tribes of the north, and for Nebuchadnezzar, the king of Babylon, my servant,

and I will bring them against the land and its inhabitants. . . . This whole land shall become a ruin and a waste, and these nations shall serve the king of Babylon seventy years" (Jeremiah 25:1-11).

God's throne on Zion had been overturned. The typical kingdom of God had passed away. Babylon had finally reached the pinncale as the Third World Power, by God's permission. At the complete desolation of Jerusalem, "the appointed times of the nations" [Gentile rule] began in the seventh lunar month of 607 B.C.* The length of time that it would span was already foreordained by the God of prophecy. Carefully examine Ezekiel's words:

"Off with his diadem, away with his crown! says the Lord the Eternal; turn things upside down, up with the low, down with the high! I lay all in ruins, ruins, ruins; everything shall be overturned, till the rightful man arrives—and I will give him everything" (Ezekiel 21:26, 27).

An important first key to understanding is introduced by Ezekiel in this text. At the climatic end of "the appointed times of the nations," *the rightful man* [Shiloh] *will be given the crown and the scepter* "that he may reign amid his foes" [Psalms 110:1, 2 and Luke 21:24]. By his own decision, God ceased to rule Israel through his reigning king at Jerusalem. The second key of interpretation, and equally significant, is the fact that God's Kingdom over any part of the earth was thus suspended, and its re-establishment must be

---

*The determination of the date of Jerusalem's destruction is highly controversal; however, careful examination verifies the accuracy to the point of usage. *The Encyclopaedia Britannica* asserts that Cyrus the Great overthrew the Babylonia dynasty in 539 B.C. According to Ezra, it was the second year, or 537 B.C., that the temple rebuilding began. Since Jeremiah spoke of a seventy-year desolation, the reversal of time from 537 B.C. would confirm the seventh month [Tishri] of the year 607 B.C.

spiritual, not fleshly, because the king to be will be raised in the Spirit.

A symbolic vision was given to King Nebuchadnezzar by God that would become the third key relating to the length of the Gentile times. It spoke of an enormous tree that an angel from heaven commanded to be chopped down. The earthly creatures were cleared out from under it, and only the *stump* of the tree remained in the ground, banded with iron and copper. It had to stay that way "among the grass of the field" until *seven times* passed over it. The prophecy further reports:

> "Let its heart be changed from that of mankind,
> and let the heart of a beast be given to it, and let
> seven times pass over it" (Daniel 4:16).

Literally, it symbolized Nebuchadnezzar who had become self-exalted to the point that he viewed his power as "reaching into the heavens." He was forced from his elevated position and debased to the state of a beast. His insanity lasted for seven times [seven years], and at the end of that time, he was obliged to confess that the Most High God was the supreme one of the universe and *gives the kingdom to whom he wants.*

When one takes account of the entire book of Daniel, it reveals that the element of time is critical in the prophecies it presents. Nebuchadnezzar was a symbol for world domination; therefore, the nation that would rule during the "appointed times" would do so without interference from God. The Gentile world rulers would exercise the dominancy that really belongs to the royal line of King David. At the end of seven times, the royal stump will be unbanded, and from its roots a new tree of rulership will emerge.

The Bible measures by lunar time, so a lunar year was reckoned as 360 days. Revelation 12:6, 14 speaks of "three and a half times" as 1,260 days. Therefore, seven times [years] would be twice that amount, or 2,520 days. In the greater fulfillment, the seven literal years had to be a measurement that would extend far into the future.

Ezekiel, who prophesied at the same time as Daniel, was inspired to give a divine rule for calculating time. He asserted, "A day for a year, a day for a year, is what I have given you" (Ezekiel 4:6). This method of computation was nothing new to the nation of Israel. Moses sent out twelve chieftains to search out the land of Canaan. Upon their return, ten of the spies gave a faithless report, and Israel believed them. God calculated the extended period they would wander in the wilderness. "By the number of days that you spied out the land, forty days, a day for a year, a day for a year, you will answer for your errors" (Numbers 14:34). By the same principle, the seven times or "times of the Gentiles" amounts to 2,520 years. The count of time began from the destruction of Jerusalem in 607 B.C., and extends 2,520 years to the year of 1914 A.D.

There are religious people who cling to that year as an important clue to the time of the end. Whether you adhere to their beliefs or concepts has nothing in common with the prophetic reality. The time proved to be crucial in the proceeding three chapters of this book, and evidence will confirm that mankind is living within a generation that will experience the climax of a world.

Many historians, analyst and prominent political figures have also alleged that 1914 was a decisive time in human history. Even after World War II had completed a half decade of bloodshed, many referred back to 1914 as a turning point in the history of the world.

> "It is indeed the year 1914 rather than that of Hiroshima which marks the turning point in our time." Rene Albrecht-Carrie of The Scientific Monthly.

> "In 1914, the world, as it was known and accepted then, came to an end." James Cameron in his book, "1914."

148

"The Great War became a pivotal moment in modern Western history. It did more than decimate a generation; it changed the world." The Boston Sunday Globe.

"It is instructive to compare the first World War with the second . . . the first war marked a far greater change in history." British historian H. R. Trevor-Roper.

"Before 1914 when there was real peace, quiet and security on this earth, there was a time we didn't know fear." Former chancellor of West Germany Konrad Adenauer.

"The whole world really blew up about World War I and we still don't know why . . . Utopia was in sight. There was peace and prosperity. Then everything blew up." Dr. Walker Percy of the American Medical News.

"Civilization entered on a cruel and perhaps terminal illness in 1914." Frank Peters of the St. Louis Post Dispatch.

"Everything would get better and better. This was the world I was born in. . . . Suddenly, unexpectedly, one morning in 1914, the whole thing came to an end." British statesman, Harold Macmillan.

"More and more historians look back upon World War I as the great turning point of modern history, the catastrophic collapse which opened the way for others, perhaps the final one." Professor D. F. Fleming of Vanderbilt University. "War has never been easy to explain and World War I is perhaps the hardest of all. Beneath the dry accounts of rivalries and alliances which historians use to explain the war, there lies a sense of something far greater, a sense of restlessness troubling the world." Barry Renfrew of the Associated Press.

"Never before had so many countries and such large armies faced each other in such gigantic battles; never had such high proportions of combatants been killed or maimed; never had man gone to war with such powerful weapons. . . . The blood and tears of the First World War changed the face of the earth." French General Richard Thoumin.

"The world has never been the same since World War I. It is useless to argue now the rights and wrongs of that catasthropic moment. All we know is that it was a turning point, and the wonderful, calm, attractive world of yesterday had vanished, never again to appear." Randolph Churchill.

Before we consider the outstanding confirmation of the year 1914 and further evidence that we are living toward the end of the appointed generation, it would be advantageous to disclose two additional points that could facilitate a better understanding of Jesus' relevance to our day.

It is significant to recall that the major cause of the two wars was attributed to the intense nationalism of the masses. This was closely associated with the self-consciousness of the majority and ironically could be traced, in greater part, to so-called Christianity. Secondly, we should consider that the science which made possible the weapons with which the wars were fought was indebted to that same agency. In contrast with the Christian principle of a self-giving love, the world inculcated hatred and utilized lies in its propaganda that seemed to serve its ends.

During the typical fulfillment of the prophecy uttered by Christ in 33 A.D., the Jewish system was destroyed with 1,100,000 Jews killed in Jerusalem alone. Many of Jesus' early disciples had died by that time; however, a remnant of the generation that witnessed his mighty works were alive to see the end of that conclusion. Four of these followers probably recalled the time Jesus was alone, and they approached him in perplexity and asked for a sign:

> "While he was sitting upon the Mount of Olives, the disciples approached him privately, saying: Tell us, when will these things be, and what will be the sign of your presence and of the conclusion of the system of things?" (Matthew 24:3).

In relation to the "great tribulation," and inclusive of Armageddon, Jesus indicated that "just as the days of Noah were, so the presence of the Son of man will be." It was clear that the approaching world destruction that would exceed the flood of Noah in proportion is associated with his presence. This thought is foreign to most of Christendom's denominations, but as brought out previously, their traditions overstep the Word of God and "for all their seeing they may not perceive, and for all their hearing they may not understand." (Mark 4:12).

In the question presented to Jesus, a most interesting prediction was unveiled. The key word was "presence" from the Greek word "par•ou•si'a." It is formed from "pa•ra'" [with] and "ou•si'a" [being], thus literally meaning, "a being with." The translations that employ the term "coming" use it on the basis for the expression "second coming," or "second advent." Most lexicographers generally acknowledge that the *presence* of the person is the main idea conveyed by the word. It is used in Youngs Literal Translation, *The Emphasized Bible* by Rotherham, and *The Emphatic Diaglott* by Wilson and James Moffatt who exert the word "arrival." By providing a *sign*, Jesus added the testimony of a second witness to pinpoint 1914 as "the end of the Gentile times" and his presence. It's ironic that many religious leaders claim the intervention of Christ

151

in their lives yet refuse to admit to his invisible manifestation.

Nearly 2,000 years ago, the anointed king made his appearance before the religious leaders of that time. They fell short in reading the signs and missed the reality of the futuristic Kingdom that Jesus spoke of. Today in lieu of the same failures, the religious figureheads completely overlook *the establishment of God's Kingdom in heaven* and continue to observe their own misconceptions as the Jews before them. Jesus' words are irrefutable when he asserts "a little longer and the world will behold me no more" (John 14:19). This Kingdom is what most involved people long for when they pray "thy Kingdom come, thy will be done, on earth as it is in heaven." This would be impossible before its establishment because Satan had access to the heavens, as indicated in the days of Job. But changes were forthcoming.

Turning to the twelfth chapter of Revelation, we read that after the birth of the Kingdom, "war broke out in heaven: Michael and his angels battled with the dragon, and the dragon with his angels battled but it did not prevail, neither was a place found for them any longer in heaven. So down the great dragon was hurled, the original serpent, the one called Devil and Satan, who is misleading the entire inhabited earth; he was hurled down to the earth and his angels were hurled down with him. . . . On this account, "Be glad you heavens and you who reside in them! Woe for the earth and for the sea, because the Devil has come down to you, having great anger, knowing he has a short period of time" (Revelation 12:7-12).

After the immense image of metallic proportions was disclosed to Daniel and its destruction thereafter, the establishment of the Kingdom, while earth's kingdoms are still in existence, is described with unmistakable clarity:

"And in the days of those kings the God of heaven will set up a Kingdom that will never be brought to ruin. And the Kingdom itself will not be passed on to any other people. It will crush and put an end to all these kingdoms [Armageddon] and it itself will stand to time indefinite" (Daniel 2:44).

When the Logos [Word] returned to heaven after his resurrection, he did not commence his rule as king. David's writings vividly describe his time of waiting when he informs us that "the man [Jesus] offered one sacrifice for sins perpetually and sat down at the right hand of God, from then on *awaiting* until his enemies should be placed as a stool for his feet" (Psalm 110:1). When the appointed time arrived [1914] for the installation of the King, David reiterates Daniel's forecast when God told his Son to "go subduing *in the midst* of your enemies" (Psalm 110:2).

We constantly hear of the *problems* that plague this world such as war, famine, diseases, natural catastrophes, etc., and fail to realize that *these are the results of the real problem*. The problem (Satan) is invisible, and no matter what man's efforts may be to deter this mishap of imperfection, only God's Kingdom can reverse the situation when his will is finally realized on earth as it has been established in heaven.

Jesus told the early Christians to exercise patience until his presence is manifested and gave them multiple evidences in a composite sign with at least thirty-nine distinct features. Mankind's history has always been one of violence and wars. Therefore, in Biblical and secular history are found hundreds of conflicts fought even prior to Jesus' day. So Jesus indicated that it was nothing new to humankind in general:

"You are going to hear of wars and reports of wars; see that you are not terrified. For these things must take place, but the end is not yet" (Matthew 24:6).

For the disciples to fully appreciate the meaning of these words, the outset of the composite sign would have to speak

153

of something that was totally different than just "wars and reports [rumors] of wars." Jesus did not disappoint them as he continued his prophetic analysis:

> "For nation will rise against nation and kingdom against kingdom, and there will be food shortages and earthquakes in one place after another. All these things are a beginning of the pangs of distress" (Matthew 24:7, 8).

He spoke of a total war that would be the greatest disaster that ever befell civilization.

Nation Against Nation

World War I was the most destructive war up to that time in human history. The nations that fought in the international conflict numbered over 65 million men directly involved in the hostility. There were over 9 million killed in action, 22 million wounded and 5 million missing. About 10 million civilians died of starvation, pestilence or decimation. The estimated costs of all the combatants and property loss is the stupendous sum of $400,000,000,000.

In adhering to Jesus' words that war and its associate sufferings would only be the "beginning of pangs of distress," the world soon gravitated into even a greater war. World War II left some 22 million dead and 34 million wounded, with an estimated cost of over $1,300,000,000,000. The peace that momentarily came in 1945 proved to be a visionary deception. Men have fought since that time in almost every corner of the earth. It is reported by the U.S. State Department that there have been, at the most, 702 million persons involved in wars of one kind or another. About 250 thousand combatants and up to 2 million civilians are dying in these wars every year. It is intimated that only twenty-five days of peace have ensued since the United Nations was formulated in 1945. Today, in this nuclear age, the Arms Control and Disarmament Agency of the United States stated that they are currently spending about one million dollars each minute on armaments. Stock piles of nuclear weapons are now equivalent in destructive power to one million atom bombs that destroyed Hiroshima. Rather than re-establishing order in the world, political powers have taken the violence of the many senseless rivalries and sealed it as the permanent condition of our century.

Food Shortages

Boundless, unlimited, inexhaustible and immeasurable are words that are used habitually in the present deliberation about the earth and its resources. Propagandists utilize them with increasing frequency in an effort to preclude the masses from recognizing the truth about man's limitations. As soon as reality surfaces, they are left with heart-corroding poverty and wide-spread hunger. The worst food shortages in human history followed the climax of the Great War. This is because famines have been characteristically man-made with war the potent cause.

Just as Jesus predicted, on the heels of the conflict of 1914, a still more frightful disaster was brewing for the entire inhabited earth. With an unusual drought sweeping the land in 1921, Russia experienced the most terrible famine in the whole recorded history of man. Millions perished while many ate hay and inexpressible filth. Men dug in graveyards and became cannibals. Great areas were depopulated which also resembled the major famine that occurred in northern China about the same time. Some 15,000 persons died every day from starvation, causing an agonizing death to an estimated 3 million inhabitants. In 1933, another 5 million perished to score the U.S.S.R. in a second famine.

The shortage of food was even greater after the World War II. A fourth of the world was plagued with food shortages. The war brought starvation to Poland, Greece and Holland and a major occurrence in Bengal, India, where 1,500,000 died. Only a blind optimist would think that this summation is complete. Half the population of the world consists of peasants struggling to produce food against the uncertainties of primitive agriculture, and this in an age of incredible scientific achievements. More recently, severe famine was recorded in Zaire, Nigeria, Somalia, Ethiopia, Thailand, Nicaragua, Pakistan, Honduras and the Sudan.

The New York Times in 1967 stated, "every 8.6 seconds some one in an underdeveloped country dies from starvation as a result of illness caused by malnutrition." Much of the world's ills can be attributed to the effects of famine. Psychologically, the mind is dominated by a desire for food. Other emotions are dulled, and there is mental anxiety. Moral standards decline, and this may be intensified by social circumstances. Epidemics of infectious diseases add greatly to the death toll in famines. It has caused a breakdown in the family unit and disrupted community living. There are now more people desperately scavenging for food than at any other time in history. Jesus' prophecy with regard to food shortages has been unquestionably fulfilled in our day. But as with wars, it is not direct proof that this generation is the one that will experience the end of our present civilization. It is only another feature of the composite sign.

Earthquakes in Diverse Places

During the past seventy years, the common occurrence of destructive earthquakes of great size has been afflicting mankind. The record continues to this day, with earthquakes repeatedly striking in different parts of the earth. Major earthquakes have averaged more than one a year since 1960. Statistics, however, show that for the 2,000 years men have been recording earthquakes up until 1914, some 4,700 lives were lost each year. But since 1914, earthquakes have taken an average of 24,000 lives annually. The following table illustrates that we are in the significant time that Jesus foretold:

Prominent Earthquakes

Year	Location	Deaths
1915	Italy	29,970
1920	China	180,000
1923	Japan	142,807
1927	China	200,000
1932	China	70,000
1934	India	10,700
1935	Pakistan	60,000
1939	Chile	30,000
1939	Turkey	23,000
1948	Japan	5,100
1949	Ecuador	6,000
1960	Morocco	12,000
1960	Chile	5,700
1962	Iran	10,000
1963	Libya	300
1964	Alaska	131
1968	Iran	11,588
1970	Peru	66,794
1970	Turkey	1,240
1971	Los Angeles	64
1972	Iran	5,374
1972	Nicaragua	10,000
1973	Mexico	527
1974	Pakistan	5,200
1975	Turkey	2,314
1976	Gualtemala	22,778
1976	China	655,000
1976	Philippines	3,300
1976	Turkey	3,700
1976	Italy	1,340
1976	Indonesia	1,048
1977	Iran	520
1977	Romania	1,541
1978	Iran	25,000
1979	Iran	196
1979	Yugoslavia	129
1980	Algeria	20,000
1980	Italy	3,000
1981	Iran	3,000
1981	Iran	1,300
1982	Yemen	2,000
1982	El Salvadore	114
1983	Columbia	250
1983	Japan	81
1983	Turkey	1,350
1983	Guinea	428
1984	Italy	84
1984	Russia	100
1985	Mexico	35,000

By any interpretation, we live in a generation of calamities. Earthquakes are commonplace and familiar just as death pervades man's thoughts to a greater extent than at any other time in the annals of civilization.

Pestilences

Concurrently with war, food shortages and earthquakes came pestilences in epidemic proportions. Each year, millions of people die from diseases. In the United States alone, diseases kill nearly two million persons each year. When the evidence is examined, there is no doubt that Jesus' words prove to be reliable:

> "And there will be great earthquakes, and in one place after another, pestilences and food shortages" (Luke 21:11).

Between 1918 and 1921, following World War I, the Spanish influenza stormed throughout the earth. It was reported by the *Saturday Evening Post* of September 26, 1959, that "no recorded pestilence before or since has equaled the death toll in total numbers. In those two years, an estimated 21,000,000 died of influenza-pneumonia throughout the world, some 850,000 in the United States alone." Within this generation rages a new age of pandemic. Despite the development of new vaccines, new strains of the flu virus have become evident. The Asian flu killed 57,000 people in 1957. The Hong Kong flu killed 33,000 in 1968 and 1969. Nearly 500,000 Americans in the past twenty years have died from the flu.

The cancer death rate accelerated in 1972 at the fastest pace in twenty-two years. It is estimated that some 850,000 new cases will be reported in 1986. At the same time, some 450,000 people will die of cancer. The number one killer, related to heart disease, strikes down an average of 550,000 annually within the boundaries of the United States.

Epidemics of polio, cholera and typhoid occur periodically, with venereal disease reaching unmanageable levels. Now, a penicillin-resistant form of gonorrhea is spreading rapidly, with the newcomer, genital herpes, affecting some 20 million people in this country alone. AIDS, the epidemic of the 1980's, is bringing a fear to the populus that has never existed before. Nearly three-fourths of the people who were first inflicted with the disease are dead.

The World Health Organization reported over 90,000 cases of smallpox in 1973, the highest total since their eradication program began in 1967. Bangladesh, Ethiopia, Pakistan and India suffered most. River Blindness [onchocerciasis] now affects an estimated 20,000,000 people throughout Africa, Guatemala, Venezuela and Mexico. Chagas' disease, a parasitic infection, afflicted some 10 million people in South and Central America, and Lupus [systemic lupus erthematosua], a sometimes fatal disease of the immune system, distressed 800,000 to one million Americans with 85-95 percent of patients living only ten years after diagnosis.

A continuance of Jesus' prediction would include Snail Fever that already touched an estimated 200 million people in 71 countries, and multiple sclerosis, a disease of the central nervous system. It afflicted some 500,000 people in the United States, striking victims during their 20's and 30's. The enumeration is endless, and medical science is up against immovable odds to bring about a permanent solution.

The Four Horsemen

Have you noticed the impact of these four features of the composite sign upon the inhabited earth? To show that they were future to the time they were written, the apostle John, reiterates the events and focuses our attention upon the current 20th century with distinctness. The ride of the four horsemen of the apocalypse is of worldwide significance:

> "And I saw, and, look! a white horse; and the one seated upon it had a bow; and a crown was given him, and he went forth conquering and to complete his conquest" (Revelation 6:2).

When do the hideous conditions exhibited by those horsemen occur? The Revelation signifies this point because after describing the horsemen, it goes on to talk about "the great tribulation," also called the "great day of wrath of God and of the Lamb Jesus Christ" (Revelation 6:17). So the conditions represented by the horsemen must precede the complete annihilation of the present religious and political order. Most of the activity presented in this Bible book occurs during what the apostle John refers to as "the Lords day" (Revelation 1:10). Therefore, it is logical that the account would initially describe "the Lord" in some way. This fact proves to be true.

Many of the world's modern-day expounders of the Scriptures diagnose the text as applying to an antichrist that would charge throughout the earth with his counterfeit rhetoric. However, this application is completely without foundation since the Bible identifies many antichrists and not an individual world conqueror.

With reference to the King, Christ Jesus, he is shown as crowned and astride a white war mount. This is undoubtedly defined at Revelation 19:11-14 where it speaks of the one on the white horse [called the Word of God] at the grand climax of his charge to "the great day of God the Almighty." According to the prophecy, this active king would remove his enemies, and this he accomplished in part when "war broke out in heaven," and Satan was cast to the vicinity of the earth. That would place the blame for the present woes of the earth directly upon the Devil, the god of this world.

The portrayal of the other three horsemen, who ride triumphantly the same time that Jesus does, serve to prove that Christ as King is riding to victory. With remarkable accuracy, Revelation runs concurrently with Jesus' signs in relation to the time of the end:

> "And another came forth, a fiery-colored horse; and to the one seated upon it there was granted to take peace away from the earth so that they should slaughter one another; and a great sword was given him" (Revelation 6:4).

The rider depicts war, but not just ordinary "wars and rumors of wars." He is given a "great sword," and he was authorized to banish peace and bring anarchy to the entire earth. Logically, it could only concur with Matthew's description of World War I. The greatness of the sword [weapons of war] would also indicate the greatness of the type of war implements. The Germans were the first to use submarines, giant airships [Zeppelins], and eventually airplanes. This brought about the development of the machine gun, the armored tank and the demoralizing use of poison gas. True to prophecy, the "fiery-colored horse" did not cease fire after the conflict but continued wars, revolution, and civil revolts to this day. Even the development of modern and more devastating nuclear weapons has moved the earth's inhabitants relentlessly toward mass annihilation.

Since famine generally follows war, it is appropriate that John saw the third rider upon a black horse:

> "And I saw, and, look! a black horse; and the one seated upon it had a pair of scales in his hand. And I heard a voice as if in the midst of the four living creatures say: a quart of wheat for a denarius, and three quarts of barley for a denarius; and do not harm the olive and the wine" (Revelation 6:6, 7).

In plain words, it signifies that food would be limited. Rationing would be necessary, as symbolized by "a pair of scales in his hand." According to the Greek historian Herodotus, one quart of grain was the minimum amount needed to maintain a soldier successfully. Therefore, it would imply that the "denarius" would be a day's wage. It clearly describes the inflationary condition that confronts countless numbers of famished people within this generation. Many were made rich through war occupations and munitions, thus making it possible to feed their lifestyle. So in their case, the "olive oil and the wine" were not harmed. It is obviously a feature of the sign that is being fulfilled in a fear-inspiring way.

War and famine have brought about millions of deaths within the past seventy years; however, there is yet another major cause of death as portended by John:

> "And I saw, and, look! a pale horse; and the one seated upon it had the name Death. And Hades was closely following him. And authority was given them over the fourth part of the earth, to kill with a long sword and with food shortage and with deadly plague . . . " (Revelation 6:8).

The third witness to the fact that King Jesus Christ had been crowned began his desolating ride throughout the earth. The pale horse with its "deadly plague" cannot be obliterated from the history of modern times. Medical science finds itself perplexed with new strains of diseases, and the malignant diseases are affecting more and more victims, so the rider has not brought his pale horse to a halt. But all of this must happen as we approach the inevitable end.

Increase of Lawlessness

J. Edgar Hoover, former director of the Federal Bureau of Investigation, stated, " . . . since 1950, crime had increased 65 percent—four times as fast as our expanding population." Today, we find ourselves confronted with the worst era of lawlessness in the nation's history. Note that Jesus' prophecy descriptively foretold the dilemma that faces the human race:

"And because of the increasing of lawlessness the love of the greater number will cool off. But he that has endured to the end is the one that will be saved" (Matthew 24:12, 13).

The statistics of crime can be understood within the structures of injustice that are created by the dominating powers. The mental image of crime, that is generally phrased, serves to avert attention from the social injustice that those with power inflict upon the masses. No political regime or system of laws has rendered a country exempt from crimes.

The rising trend has not come on the scene over a long period of time. It has been gathering pace since World War I, with the speed of growth unimitated before that marked year. Homicide, rape and robbery have all taken a sharp upward turn in the last two decades. These trends are real and cannot be accounted for merely in terms of the increasing population. On the average, a serious crime is committed about every second in the United States alone.

New threats of international crime have surfaced in the last half of the twentieth century. Drug trafficking, skyjacking and political terrorism are beyond the effective control of any one nation. Wherever you will look on this earth, terrorism is dangerously present. Terrorists have overthrown democracies. Thousands have died as a result of terrorist feuding between Catholics and Protestants in Northern Ireland. In Japan, militant terrorists delayed the opening of Tokyo's new international airport for five years. Palestinian guerrillas continue to fight against Israel; however, no nation or individual is immune to their radical, swinish behavior. *The U.S. News Report* of May 22, 1978, describes the situation as an "epidemic of violence."

World Fear

In describing the heavy cloud of fear that hovers over the present world, Jesus emphatically declares:

"Also there will be signs in sun and moon and stars, and on the earth anguish of nations, not knowing the way out because of the roaring of the sea and its agitation, while men become faint out of fear and expectation of the things coming upon the inhabited earth; for the powers of the heaven will be shaken" (Luke 21:25, 26).

Already, mental pain and the feeling of defenselessness have taken hold of mankind as they confront a dismal and meaningless future. What the next few years may yield in the way of fearsome developments is a thought that could well push humankind closer to panic. With the atomic explosion over Japan in 1945, a new source of fear and anxiety emerged onto the world stage. The threat of nuclear war is universal. The two ideological blocs [the two kings of vexation] face each other in a subtle stalemate based on what is known as Mutual Assured Destruction, or MAD for short.

Other discoveries of modern science have caused unprecedented fear and mental distress. High-energy cosmic rays originating from an unknown source in the heavens have been found to be striking the earth in great numbers and with energy enough to penetrate hundreds of feet. Adding to the fears is the terrifying prospect of established military bases in outer space with terrorizing weapons aimed and ready to shower destruction to any location on the earth. Never before in history have men had the capabilities to end civilization by blowing the world into a desolate, radioactive wasteland. The agitation of the sea of mankind only enhances the present enigma. These threats are quantitatively and qualitatively dissimilar from those in the past.

The Notable Generation

Not to be dismissed from consideration as being a cause of man's degeneration is the letter of the apostle Paul to Timothy:

"But know this that in the last days critical times hard to deal with will be here. For men will be lovers of themselves, lovers of money, self-assuming, haughty, blasphemers, disobedient to parents, unthankful, disloyal, having no natural affection, not open to any agreement, slanderers, without self-control, fierce, without love of goodness, betrayers, headstrong, puffed up with pride, lovers of pleasure rather than lovers of God, having a form of godly devotion but proving false to its power" (2 Timothy 3:1-5).

The critical times have been spawned by the insurgent condition that Paul described. The results are the appalling state of affairs that we discern in government, business, religion, and in the oppositional human society. Greed has become a stationary condition in the lives of the wavering multitude. Never before has a generation of people displayed such a materialistic tendency. At their disposal is an abundance of material possessions and comfort, and this greed is exploited by advertisers' claims that these things are absolute necessities for complete gratification. The "love of money" and of "self" have become a gauge for measuring happiness.

Rather than discussing the external forces that affected mankind, Paul emphasizes the attitudes of people who experience these dramatic events. Prior to the outbreak of World War I, the family roles and the responsibilities of each family member were clearly defined; however, the lifestyle was drastically changed due to the demoralizing influences that were predicted to occur.

The present marked generation has been obsessed with their personal rights as never before. Gradually, parents have allowed their children to dispute with them and assert their own opinions, even to the extent of disobedience. It was reported that one fourth of all serious crimes in Greater London, England, are committed by school children. In the

United States, teenage arrests for violent crimes increased 293 percent between 1960 and 1975. The overall ratio of juvenile arrests is growing twice as fast as the adult generation. The young criminals have become pathological, "without self control" or "love of goodness."

Throughout the opinionated world, possessions are rated above human relationships as to importance. Often, moral and religious standards have decreased nearly to the point of being nonexistent. Not only have vast numbers of Americans lost all sense of the spiritual aspects of life, but the religious leaders are often found in the forefront of this undevout pursuit of comfort rather than implicit belief. Religion has never been poorer spiritually than it is today. The majority of the people are members of a church, but are really nonbelievers. They, in reality, "have a form of godly devotion but prove false to its power."

Days that are labeled "the last days" will eventually have an end. Jesus' prophecies of Matthew, Chapters 24 and 25, Mark, Chapter 13, and Luke, Chapter 21 were limited to a particular time when the final tally was to be expected. Space does not permit further details of man's contempt for God's laws, but what has been presented clearly shows that since 1914, events have been moving the world toward the Day the Lion Roars. We are living in a judgemental generation as Matthew explicitly outlines. The course a person chooses during this time determines the outcome of his very existence. The Gospel writer stated that "when the Son of man [Christ] arrives in his glory, and all the angels with him, then he will sit down on his glorious throne [1914], and the nations will be gathered before him, and he will separate people one from another, just as a shepherd separates the sheep from the goats. And he will put the sheep on his right hand, but the goats on his left" (Matthew 25:31-46).

For further edification, Jesus reinforces the composite sign with this remarkable feature:

"Truly I say to you that this generation will by no

means pass away until all these things occur"
(Matthew 24:34).

It does not relate to a period of time as 70, 80, or even 100 years. Rather, it refers to the people who were living at the beginning of the "pangs of distress." This was the generation that observed the events that suddenly led to World War I. *The U. S. News Report* of January 14, 1980, made an important observation. They stated that "10 is the age at which an event creates a lasting impression on a person's memory." If this be the case, then there were nearly 12 million Americans in 1980 who were capable of having a recollection of the Great War. The fact that this generation is receding is a strong indication that the conclusion is moving fast toward its climax. With the yearly death rate prefigured using the inclining ratio from 1980 to 1985, it is calculated that by 1995, only 2,842,138 of the designated generation will still be living. If consideration is given to the fact that "the generation will by no means pass away," then one must be convinced that the end of civilization as we know it will culminate *before* the end of the 20th century and possibly much sooner than is foreseen.

In the words of instruction given to the apostles are embodied the full answer to their questions. The Scriptures reveal the most up-to-date description of events to transpire on this earth, and they have given us accurate signs to indicate his "presence" and the generation that would experience the end. It applies to our day, and with much greater force as we observe the fulfillment of all the occurrences recorded. If one adheres to 1948, when the Republic of Israel was established, or the Six Day War of 1967 as the end of the Gentile times, then his prediction has completely ignored the most devastating catastrophes ever to atomize the face of the earth. Christ knew that errors would abound in regard to this subject and prefaces his instruction with the warning, "Take care that no one misleads you." In the study of the "Stump of Seven Times" and the eventualities that followed, it is a necessity that the heart is open to the truth and not blinded by any traditional ideas or theories that will only serve to lull the people to a pathetic sleep.

Chapter 8
The Great Harlot

. . . and you offer a bribe to them to
come in to you from all around in
in your acts of prostitution.

Ezekiel 16:33

The interpretation of history is based on the scattered traces of events and the gathering of such evidences that eventually fill the archives of civilization. Though no shamanic touch can totally restore the dead past, history satisfies the inquirer as to what happened and why. What forces have been at work to move the energy of nations to create such a march of events? Why was Jerusalem devastated and what distinguishing influence did the Babylonian culture have on the religious credence of today? Was it the direct intervention of an overruling Sovereign, whose purpose was to keep the nations in motion until the appointed time? When we speak of the interpretation of history, it does not mean its setting in the universe, but a knowledge of its own inner affinity with God's scheme of arrangement and how it entwines with the mystery of this greater Babylon.

Belshazzar had already proved himself an effectual administrator in Babylon, and so Nabonidus, his father, felt himself entirely relieved to press on to other enterprises. While he was busying himself with architecture and archaeology, the most remarkable of ancient conquerors known as Cyrus the Great had arisen from Elam and entered Babylon on October 29, 539 B.C., to assume complete authority as victor. In time, Babylon decayed into the darkness of the earth. High mounds of dirt represent all that remains of the cities of Mesopotamia.

Although only the ground and traces of wall structures appear silhouetted against the sky, the desolate antiquities of a great civilization still loom in the shadows. What, then, is the Babylon spoken of by the apostle John the one referred to as "Babylon the Great, the mother of the harlots and of the disgusting things of the earth?" There are many clues in the last book of the Bible as to its identification, but since the intimation is prophetic, it is necessary to regress into the outline of time and parallel prophecy with historical facts.

The Plain of Shinar

Early in the second millennium B.C., there existed in southwest Asia an event of lasting significance for the history of man. It was then that Nimrod, the grandson of Ham, the great grandson of Noah, established a kingdom in Lower Mesopotamia which attracted the attention of the surrounding nations. Noah and his son Shem refer to the city by the name of Babel. The early Greek Septuagint translation of Genesis 11:9 call it *Sy'nkhysis* or "Confusion." The Bible presents the record in these words:

> "And this is the history of Noah's sons, Shem, Ham and Japheth. Now sons began to be born to them after the deluge. . . . And the sons of Ham were Cush and Mizraim and Put and Canaan. . . . And Cush became father to Nimrod. He made the start in becoming a mighty one in the earth. He displayed himself a mighty hunter in opposition to Yahweh. And the beginning of his kingdom came to be Babel and Erech and Accad and Calneh in the land of Shinar" (Genesis 10:1-12).

In what sense was Nimrod "a mighty hunter in opposition of Yahweh?" The more we discover about the nature of Nimrod and the influence that the Kingdom of Babylon yielded toward future civilizations, the more understanding can be drawn as to Babylon the Great and the foundation upon which it rests.

The hunting of birds for food and wild animals for clothing or protection, is sanctioned by the Bible. However, the hunting for the sake of sport or to engage in killing whimsically is condemned. Kings kept lions in cages or pits from the period of Abraham onward, but the Assyrian rulers hunted them and gloated over the prestige they received for engaging in the alluring exploit. Nimrod "the mighty hunter," was in reality an Assyrian king. Wild bulls, ostriches and even elephants were likewise searched out and many times kept in parks where the royal hunter could present his yarn of the perilous charge. Importantly, the pursuit to obtain animals for food or to reduce the number of predators on the flocks was not employed in Mesopotamia.

After the Great Flood, the Creator made it legal for mankind to eat the flesh of animals, birds and fish. But since the life of the creature which God provided had to be taken into consideration, certain restrictions were enforced. It is recorded in Genesis 9:1-6, and the words are compellingly presented:

> "And God went on to bless Noah and his sons and to say to them: Be fruitful and become many and fill the earth. And a fear of you and a terror of you will continue upon every living creature of the earth and upon every flying creature of the heavens, upon everything that goes moving on the ground, and upon all the fishes of the sea. In your hand they are now given. Every moving animal that is alive may serve as food for you. As in the case of green vegetation, I do give it all to you. Only flesh with its soul—its blood—you must not eat. And, besides that, your blood of your souls shall I ask back. From the hand of every living creature shall I ask it back; and from the hand of man, from

the hand of each one who is his brother, shall I ask back the soul of man. Anyone shedding man's blood, by man will his own blood be shed, for in God's image he made man."

After the establishment of his kingdom, Nimrod made expeditions to the north into Assur [Assyria] to build the city of Nineveh. Having achieved a position of notoriety, "the mighty hunter" rapidly increased his power and rather than hunting animals, intensified his violation against Yahweh by spilling the blood of man. Since the restriction assigned to mankind asserted that "the life of all flesh is in the blood," Nimrod became responsible. Habakkuk 2:12 reiterates this infraction by declaring "woe to the one that is building a city by bloodshed and that has solidly established a town by unrighteousness." This being prohibited to Noah appears also to have been forbidden to all mankind to this day. It was not only enjoined upon the entire nation of Israel, but the early Christians scrupulously complied to the decree pronounced by the apostles at Jerusalem "in abstaining from things strangled and from blood."

Although Noah was a family head, he did not appoint himself king over mankind. He recognized the Creator as being the Supreme One of the universe. Nimrod, on the other hand, made rapid strides to create a name for himself, even to the extent of killing his own brothers. In the Jewish interpretative translation of the Bible called "Targums," it reads that "he was powerful in hunting the sons of men," and he said to them, "Depart from the judgment of the Lord, and adhere to the judgment of Nimrod." The works entitled *Antiquities of the Jews,* by the ancient Jewish historian Flavius Josephus, says, "Now the multitude were very ready to follow the determination of Nimrod, and to esteem it a piece of cowardice to submit to God; and they built a tower." The tower or ziggurat was built as a milestone of religious worship.

Religious Inception

Religion has always greatly contributed to the life of all people in ancient times. The kings not only ruled by divine right, but they were also honored as earthly representatives of the great gods. Therefore, he who controlled the state was both king and priest. In an effort to magnify his role visually, a ziggurat was built solely to elevate the temple and shrine of the presiding deity that stood on the topmost platform, as high as possible above the king's domain. The king was exempt from taxes and received contributions from the private citizens, but chiefly from rulers who expected to win the favor of the gods. In view of this fact, the temples acquired immense wealth and became the centers not only of religious pursuits, but also of commercial endeavors.

Every important city had its great temples dedicated to its own god for whom it claimed primacy over the gods of its neighbors. This religious rivalry was a cause of incessant contention, much as the denominational separatism today. Some cities were able to subdue their neighbors and became the seats of small principalities. In order to contend with the differing religious beliefs in his settlement, Hammurabi, in the year 1764 B.C., succeeded in imposing a religious precedent which long outlasted his dynasty. This he did by the simple scheme of making Marduk, god of Babylon, into the predominant god of the Mesopotamian deities. Naturally this made Babylon the center of religion and became a unifying link to the land.

Dogmatic Openness

Man has venerated everything on earth, between the earth and heaven and everything in the heavens above. He has even revered his ancestors as well as himself. When the belief of invisible spirits succeeds that of spiritual bodies, an object becomes the abode of the spirit. Many stone monuments have become holy simply through some affiliation with the deceased or with doctrinal theology. Carved images are worshipped as eagerly with numbers made to frighten away evil spirits. The homage given to trees is one of the oldest practices. Possibly it was the entire forest rather than a single tree that received religious adoration due to it being a terrifying object. As soon as man begin to think in spiritual terms, he personified the tree and attired it in glitter. Jeremiah expresses this quite familiar custom:

"This is what Yahweh has said: Do not learn the way of the nations at all, and do not be struck with terror even at the signs of the heavens, because the nations are struck with terror at them. For the customs of the peoples are just an exhalation, because it is a mere tree out of the forest that one has cut down, the work of the hands of the craftsman with the billhook. With silver and with gold one makes it pretty. With nails and with hammers they fasten them down that none may reel" (Jeremiah 10:2-4).

The importance of trees survived the Babylonian culture. In the seventeenth century, this reverence was practiced in Europe and restricted to superstitions in regard to the use of amulets. By rapping on wood three times, it offered protection by appeasing the Trinity. Later, the tradition was connected with Christ's day or Christmas and celebrated on December 25, which was a Mithraic feast or birthday of the unconquered Sun. The transition from paganism to Christianity was by degrees but became discernible after the fall of Rome. The adoration of the cradle was borrowed from the cult of Adonis, and the cave where the child Adonis was born was adopted for the apostatized Christian Church by the Empress Helena, and later sanctioned by the pagan emperor, Constantine.

Archaeological unearthlings confirm the Bible as to how thoroughly the Chaldeans were engrossed in astrology. The prophet Isaiah spoke of Babylon's "worshippers of the heavens, the lookers at the stars, those giving out knowledge at the new moons concerning the things that will come" (Isaiah 47:12, 13). The government as well as people's personal dealings were largely directed by the "lookers at the stars," the astrologers. The star-cult spread throughout the earth. Ancient Egypt adopted the practice, and in time, it was carried to Greece. After ancient Rome defeated the Grecian Empire, it became a thriving metropolis for astrology. The deeper the Romans sank in religion and morals, the more astrology became consolidated with all activities and belief.

It is no different in this age of practicality—those who depend on astrology as their guide will come to a disastrous end. America is just one of many countries that abound with people who operate their lives by the stars. There is an estimated three million who profess Christianity and religiously run their daily lives on a celestial schedule. God's Word foretold that in these last days "some will fall away from the faith, paying attention to misleading inspired utterances and teachings of demons" (1 Timothy 4:1).

Consider, for example, the Christian festival of Easter in which the ancient fertility rites of the spring equinox are today cleverly disguised in the rabbit and the decorative colored eggs. The very name "Easter" is a distortion of the name of the great mother earth goddess Ashtoreth, and ironically, they called her the "queen of heaven" (Jeremiah 7:18). To the Greeks and the Romans, she was known as Astarte. She became merely a display of new clothes, headdresses, paint, oil, and ornamental marks assumed by savages, but now these things are employed for ritualistic ends. Solomon introduced her worship into Jerusalem, and the altars remained until the reign of Josiah in 650 B.C. (2 Kings 23:13). However, more important to this examination is that it is the restoration of the original Babylonian goddess, Istar.

The doctrine of immortality holds a very inferior place

in the Hebrew Scriptures, more commonly called the Old Testament. The Pentateuch contains no revelation of a glory to be revealed in the very presence of an incorruptible soul. Even the Son of God rebuked the Sadducees and declared they erred for not perceiving this fact. The dogma was held unfalteringly by the Babylonians who believed in a conscious existence after death. It was later expressed in the plainest terms by men like Plato and Cicero. The effects of the doctrine of Socrates and the Platonist philosophy appear to be strongly entrenched in the writings of Saint Augustine. In his book, *The City of God*, Augustine asserts that "certain partakers with us in the grace of Christ wonder when they hear and read that Plato had conception concerning God, in which they recognize considerable agreement with the truth of our religion. Therefore, we have thought it better to plead our cause with the Platonists because their writings are better known. Assuredly, Plato thinks that the souls of mortals cannot always be in their bodies, but must necessarily be dismissed by death, and from death to life." Eventually from his teachings, it was incorporated into the apostatized credence.

When one inquires as to the grounds on which such a belief rests, the answer cannot be too hastily given. It must be remembered that the soul, which according to Genesis is a combination of the body and the breath of life, loses its consciousness in sleep after death (John 11:11). The word "immortality" and related terms only appear six times in the entire Bible, and each time refers to a reward that one seeks rather than already possesses. Although this book is not for the purpose of generating doctrine, the subject must be confronted in an effort to expose the unchaste influence that was infused by the ancient religious order. Before revealing the pageantry of the Great Harlot in the prophetic vision of John, we have to consider the degradation of the nation of Israel and the hostility she experienced with the demonic and persuasive Babylonian power.

The Harlot's Counterpart

The ancient power of Babylon continued for centuries as a fount for degenerate paganism. The city was the first to claim the designation, "the eternal city." Political sovereigns came and went, yet the seat of false religion survived by means of the crafty maneuvering attained by its influential priesthood.

Although Solomon became the most glorious of the kings, he eventually abandoned the divine instructions and became entangled with foreign customs. In his old age, he was governed by the whims of his pagan marriages and turned to idol worship. In time, because of the heavy yoke placed upon the nation, a divisional breach resulted. The withdrawing ten tribes of Israel established a northern kingdom under the reign of Jeroboam, while the tribes of Judah and Benjamin, together with the Levites remained observant to David's line.

Jeroboam no longer exhibited confidence in God's promises. Fearing that his subjects would return to the house of David, he violated the covenant and coined the idolatrous worship of golden calves. He commanded his people to adopt the new state religion. Through this action, he sealed the demise of the new kingdom as well as his own rulership. The prophets foretold that God would execute his judgements upon Assyria because of all she had done to his chosen people. It is also thought-provoking that Jerusalem was permitted to witness the destruction as a preview of divine punishment.

The kingdom of Judah survived that of the house of Israel by 133 years. However, only a short twenty-four years will elapse before the covenanted house will turn their attention to Babylonian factions. Manasseh, son and successor of Hezekiah, was marked by deeds of impiety and cruelty. His influence sided with those who carried their opposition to the worship of Yahweh to such an extent that he was not permitted in Jerusalem. He, in turn, spiritually prostituted himself to the Babylonian viceroy in his revolt against Assyria. He was finally captured and was carried to Babylon as a prisoner. He sought repentance, and with his prayer answered, returned to Jerusalem where he restored worship once again.

Judah's next king, Amon, carried on a wicked and idolatrous reign for two years. His servants conspired against him and assassinated him in the palace. The people put the conspirators to death and placed his son Josiah on the throne.

The affairs of the kingdom, which must have existed during Josiah's minority, are not recorded. However, in the course of his eighteenth year, he emerges into history when he began to cleanse the entire kingdom of false worship. The tempest which shook two great powers was advantageous to the peace of Josiah's kingdom. The empire of Assyria was practically broken, and the Chaldeans were starting to develop, under Nebopolassar, into the aggressive form of a world power. A disastrous encounter took place at Megiddo between Egypt and Babylon. For reasons unknown, King Josiah led his armies out through the pass at Megeddo, and lost his crown as well as his life.

Jehoiakim [Eliakin] was made king of Judah by Necho, king of Egypt. After four years he was defeated by Nebuchadnezzar and compelled to pay tribute to him. Three years afterward, he rebelled but was taken prisoner, and finally permitted to reign as a vassal. In 618 B.C., he rebelled again, thus forcing Nebuchadnezzar to come against Jerusalem the second time. Jehoiakim died inside Jerusalem but was dragged beyond the gates and left unattended. This was when Daniel and his companions were taken into exile (Daniel 1:1).

Jehoiachin, his son, reigned only three months and ten days when he was taken captive, so in 617 B.C., Zedekiah [Mattaniah] became the final vassal king of Judah. Jeremiah's astonishing prophecy foretelling the fall of Babylon caused Zedekiah to react rebelliously toward the king; however, about the same time another prophet was raised up who predicted the destruction of Jerusalem.

Visions of Fornication

Ezekiel was exiled to Babylon, but unlike Jeremiah, he did not directly experience the detestable practices within the walls of Jerusalem. In vision, he penetrated through the temple wall and "portrayed upon the wall round about, were all kinds of creeping things, and loathsome beasts and all the idols of the house of Israel." He then noticed "seventy men of the elders" who were offering incense to the carvings (Ezekiel 8:1-12). At the entrance of the "north gate of the house of the LORD," he envisioned "women weeping over Tammuz [Alorus], the god of fire (Ezekiel 8:13, 14).

Besides such detestable idolatrous worship, they likewise played the harlot by entering into relationship with the nations of the world that they may gain popularity and influence. Unlike the prostitute who received gifts for services, Jerusalem is accused of committing the perverted act of paying men to cohabit with her (Ezekiel 16:33, 34). It was no surprise, therefore, that the prophet hears the call of Yahweh's executioners to kill everyone not marked. "Pass through the city and smite; slay old men, young men and maidens, little children and women, but touch no one upon whom is the mark" (Ezekiel 9:5, 6).

The King of Babylon burnt the temple and the entire city of Jerusalem, thus disgorging the land of Judah as "an empty vessel, turning it upside down and leaving nothing inside" (Jeremiah 51:34). He broke down the walls of the city and confiscated what silver and gold was left in the temple, and all the instruments of brass. It was the end of the magnificent earthly kingdom of Israel. It could have been more glorious so that it could have attracted all nations to know and serve the true God; however, the transgressions of both the kings and the people of Israel averted this, and God permitted their polity to suffer destruction.

The inhumanity that was executed by Nebuchadnezzar and the Chaldean army made him and his domain blood-guilty. The remnant of Zion had good reason for expressing a stately prayer to God to retaliate because of the Jewish blood that was spilled at Jerusalem. The one authorized under the Mosaic Law to avenge the blood of one who had been killed was called the "avenger of blood" or go'el,' and was the nearest male relative (Numbers 35:19). Inasmuch as the ancient nation of Israel was bound to God by means of a Law Covenant, Yahweh was their "husbandly owner," and as such, the go'el' (Jeremiah 3:14).

Jerusalem had a valid case against Babylon before the supreme court of the universe. Jeremiah recorded:

> "Therefore thus says the LORD: Behold, I will plead your cause and take vengeance for you. I will dry up her sea and make her fountain dry; and Babylon shall become a heap of ruins, the haunt of jackals, a horror and a hissing, without inhabitants" (Jeremiah 51:36, 37).

After prophesying, Jeremiah inserted a divine warning that was to reoccur in the final revelation of the Christ. With the predicted deliverer Cyrus in mind, he said, " . . . go out of the midst of her, my people! Let every man save his life from the fierce anger of the LORD." All this exaltation and primacy of the Babylonian authority finally underwent a drastic trembling when the empire politically fell at the hands of Cyrus the Great. The Bible indicates that the Babylonian priesthood survived and settled in Pergamum, an Asian province just west of the depleted hierarchy.

Babylon the Great

The inhabitants of ancient Babylon mirrored the surety of the rulers. They felt protected because of their military and politico-economical strength. Babylon was the "eternal city" and the pride of the entire world. Although the fortified city seemed inpregnable, the strange words of Jeremiah continued to sound the warning to "flee from the midst of her; let every man save his life! Be not cut off in her punishment, for this is the time of the LORD'S vengeance, the requital he is rendering her" (Jeremiah 51:6).

This provocative ancient profile is not dead history, but rather a prophetic reality that lives for today and finds its parallel today. All of these things have tremendous impact upon the religious realm of the twentieth century. Literal Babylon proved to be a boastful possession of God's adversary, and it came to represent all the unsavory works that are a symbol of Babylon the Great. In his first letter, the apostle John stated, " . . . the whole world is lying in the power of the wicked one." He then reiterates this apostate influence in his dynamic prophecy of worldwide religionism.

"And upon her forehead was written a name, a mystery: Babylon the Great, the mother of the harlots and of the disgusting things of the earth" (Revelation 17:5).

In ancient Babylon where false religion was first predicated, prostitution was a dominant part of the religious observance. Every female was requested to relinquish her virginity at the temple of Ishtar, goddess of fertility. The state treasury was enlarged considerably with the monies paid by the devout male participants. They were conditioned in the public prayers to request the gods to pluralize their prostitutes because the commercial use of them was neither thought of as sinful or disgraceful. How different was the law given to the nation of Israel! The words emphatically asserted to the people to "not profane your daughters by making them prostitutes, in order that the land may not commit prostitution and the land actually be filled with loose morals" (Leviticus 19:29).

Spiritual prostitution is a person, a nation or a denomination of persons who allege that they are consecrated to God, but who make alliances with the world or turn to a form of pagano-Christianism. The most inglorious of this degeneration is "Babylon the Great." James addresses these apostates as "adultresses" and asks, " . . . do you not know that friendship with the world is enmity with God? Therefore, whoever wants to be a friend of the world is constituting himself an enemy of God" (James 4:4). The "world" here, as in many places throughout the Bible, has reference to humans in general who are not serving God, but are "lying in the power of the wicked one." A Christian is expected to remain free from the violence and corruption of the world, not partaking of its political divergence or its nationalistic platform of hatred.

The essential source of material that identifies The Great Harlot is the characterization given by the apostle John. Consider the enclosures:

> "One of the seven angels who had the seven bowls came and said to me, Come, I will show you the punishment of the great prostitute, who sits on many waters. With her the kings of the earth committed adultery and the inhabitants of the earth were intoxicated with the wine of her adulteries.' The waters you saw, where the prostitute sits, are people, multitudes, nations and languages. The woman you saw is the great city that rules over the kings of the earth. . . . The merchants who sold these things and gained their wealth from her will stand far off, terrified at her torment they will weep and mourn" (Revelation 17:1, 2, 15, 18; 18:15).

Interference in the political arena is true not only with the denominations of Christendom, but also the so-called pagan religions of the Middle and Far East. It has been estimated that over half of the world's population professes affiliation with some religious order. However, the appalling statistics reveal that the fruits of God's Spirit are not manifested in public life. The physician Luke expounded this reality in his allusive phrase of salvation:

> "Exert yourselves vigorously to get in through the narrow door, because *many*, I tell you, will seek to get in but will not be able" (Luke 13:24).

Many sensationalistic scholars assume that Revelation is speaking of a politico-religious system that will manifest itself in the city of Babylon or Rome. Hal Lindsey in his book, *The Late Great Planet Earth*, made an inventive observation when he implied, " . . . this harlot . . . is not only a system but also a city. There is no question about where the city would be—it was Rome!"

History has already shown that Babylon as a political system had long ceased to exist. As to Rome, the essence of its political power does not conform with the depiction of Babylon the Great's course and its scheme of domination. She is a prostitute, "the kings of the earth committed adultery with her, and by her magic spell, all the nations were led astray" (Revelation 18:3, 23). Literal Rome's supremacy was procured by military strength, where Babylon's domination was by reason of idolatries. Thus, the idea that Babylon means Rome is simply an interpretation of random logic, and is not supported by fact.

The Bible assures us that the Lord God does nothing without revealing his secret to his servants, the prophets (Amos 3:7). Having advanced knowledge from God, those who desire to know of his divine plan are prepared to perceive the identity of the Great Harlot and how the great tribulation is actually brought about by her demise. *At this very moment,* events are unfolding that are readying the way for that execution.

Since the kings were to have spiritual intercourse with her, it is evident that this "Babylon the Great" cannot be another political monarch. Ancient Babylon was known for its apostate religion and emplaces the Great Harlot as the representation of *a worldwide empire of apostate religion.* The "Man of Lawlessness" would unquestionably be the controlling factor of the compromising immorality with the world, rather than presenting herself as a virgin espoused to Christ as head. The nations are led astray because of her "magic spell" or spiritistic practices. The majority of this world's population, whether a participant with the many religious entities or supporters of the worldly political establishments, are captives of the Great Harlot and her political paramours. The masses are hardened to the present corrupt state of affairs and may find it difficult to conceive that world religion is responsible for this immoral dilemma, but the facts are incontestable.

In Revelation, Chapter 17, the apostle John is reported as seeing the composite figure that represents the complete number of earthly kings that sensuously associate with the Babylonian harlot:

> "Then the angel carried me away in the spirit into a desert. There I saw a woman sitting on a scarlet beast that was covered with blasphemous names and had seven heads and ten horns" (Revelation 17:3).

With the vast prophetic knowledge that is available in this time of the end, there is no mystery as to the identity of the "scarlet beast." Except for the skin color, the scarlet beast is very similar to the seven-headed beast as identified in the chapter Seven Heads of Predominance. It is the look-alike *image* or the *United Nations.* This image reflects the flaws and imperfections of the world's political systems. Review the description a second time:

> "The wild beast that you saw was [League of Nations], but is not [fell in 1939], and yet is about to ascend out of the abyss [United Nations], and it is to go off into destruction. And when they see how the wild beast was, but is not, and yet will be present, those who dwell on the earth will wonder

admiringly, but their names have not been written upon the scroll of life from the founding of the world" (Revelation 17:8).

Babylon the Great engaged in further immorality with the composite beast in that she venerated this image as the expression of God's Kingdom on earth. As a result of wine-bibbing from her cup and because of her relationship with the political element, the people undergo adversities through religious wars, economic repression, abased morality, illiteracy, and an absence of faith. Her membership has produced spirit mediums, foretune-tellers and astrologers, and has cultivated and upheld the works of the flesh such as obscene practices, prostitution, homosexuality, loose conduct and drunkenness.

In addition, the worldwide religious order has prospered with commercial endeavors. Today, as ancient Babylon thrived from the Euphrates River and the commerce it yielded, the Harlot sits on the broad waters of peoples and nations and experiences a materialistic benefit by means of such waters. They have not even hesitated to become involved with racketeers and revolutionaries in their pursuit of wealth.

More than that, Babylon the Great has become drunk in human blood, especially in the many wars that were fought in the name of Christianity. For centuries she has brought dishonor upon God and his Christ by devastating crusades, demonic inquisitions and the massive slaughter that has plagued humankind since World War I. She continues to set astride the beastlike world confederation of governments, but not for long. Her extermination is just as certain as the destruction that befell ancient Jerusalem, as well as her subjects of whom possess the mark of the beast. John deliberates this symbolic recognition:

"He also forced everyone, small and great, rich and poor, free and slave, to receive a mark on his right hand or on his forehead, so that no one could buy or sell unless he had the mark, which is the name of the beast or the number of his name. This calls for wisdom. If anyone has insight, let him calculate the number of the beast, for it is man's number. His number is 666" (Revelation 13:16-18).

This text and number have been misinterpreted in many ways and each time with a mysterious connotation. In his book, *The 1980's: Countdown to Armageddon*, the author implies, " . . . those worshipers will each be assigned a trade number. Without that number, no one will be permitted to buy or sell anything." This shallow notion violates all rules of interpretation and does not depend upon insight. In the Scriptures, the number six is a symbol of incompleteness or as "man's number," imperfection. Satan's visible organization consists of three basic ruling elements—political, religious and the commercial faction. The number 666 could well illustrate the three components; however, the meaning is straightforward. The number three is used at times to denote intensity or emphasis [Compare Ezekiel 21:27, Matthew 26:34, Acts 10:16, Revelation 4:8]. The imperfections and inadequacy of the beast were only emphasized by raising the number six to the third degree.

In John's vision, the mark on the forehead publicly designates one as a worshiper of the scarlet beast, thus granted exclusive privileges. Jesus stresses this point when he stipulated that, " . . . if you were a part of the world, the world would be fond of what is its own" (John 15:19). The mark in the hand would reasonably signify incisive support of the wild beast, as with working with the hands.

As far as her ruination, the Bible says that "her plagues shall come in a single day, in one hour" (Revelation 18:8, 10). It will be very similar to what happened to ancient

Babylon, which "fell in one night." This execution is clearly portrayed in John's record:

"The beast and the ten horns you saw will hate the prostitute. They will bring her to ruin and leave her naked; they will eat her flesh and burn her with fire" (Revelation 17:16).

Church criticism of the state is growing as the system approaches its climax. In the United States, many religions support lobbyists right in the nation's capital in an effort to sway lawmakers. This type of lobbying has existed for a long time with prudence. The recent phenomenon—and much less discreet—has been the egress of special interest groups organized by Protestant fundamentalists. World leaders have cultivated a practice to not underestimate their influence.

The World Council of Churches became implicated in state polity in a less subtle way. Since 1970 the Council has contributed millions of dollars to various political revolutionary crusades. This has amassed a frightful blood debt before God and has polluted the masses with religious hatred.

Again, some religious leaders seek elective office in government. This is expected to organize even greater pressure groups in order to promote programs that are important to them. Religious leaders get involved in political affairs because they want to set a moral tone or warn when governments take the wrong path, but in the process, they take the wrong path themselves. The Bible clearly cautions Christians to "not avenge yourselves, . . . for it is written: Vengeance is mine; I will repay" (Romans 12:19).

Acts of interference only weakens the moral lead that religions are trying to incorporate. Some religionists encourage disarmament, while others pray for their country to have the most powerful military force since creation. The Moral Majority works for the survival of America along with its capitalistic mode. How is the outsider to know which course is considered the moral standard when leaders give disagreeing opinions? This does nothing to relieve world tension.

By intruding in the political arena, organized religion is tolling their own death knell. It may be time for concerned persons to take offensive against those elements in religion that have crossed the line separating legitimate critics from enemies of the state, because the harlot is to be executed by the political elements that have carried on immoral intercourse with her. It is not for reasons of jealousy, but because she had deceived them. She had created a world situation that makes the controlling of such an impossibility. They come to the point of hatred that causes them to want to obliterate all thoughts of her existence. As ancient Babylon surmised, so Babylon the Great views the prediction as completely unbelievable, but what she fails to understand is "God has put it into their hearts to accomplish his purpose" (Revelation 17:17).

True to prophecy, the figurative waters of millions of

people are withdrawing their support and have decidedly weakened the religious element. The waters in effect are drying up. It fits the apostle Paul's description of the "last days" when it indicated that people would be "lovers of pleasure rather than lovers of God." John proclaims the disquieting warning for righteously inclined persons to "Get out from her, my people, if you do not want to share with her sin, and if you do not want to receive part of her plagues" (Revelation 18:4). The harlot's destruction will ignite the beginning of the great tribulation. Of course, when the scarlet beast turns on the harlot, they will be drawing near to the time of their own destruction during The Day the Lion Roars.

How obvious that Babylon the Great is a worldwide religious empire. In the Bible, no priests are mentioned in connection with the Great Harlot because she herself stands for apostate religion. A decision must be made sometimes. A decision must be handed down by a competent judge and must be executed. Things cannot indefinitely continue as they are. Man's plain common sense can see that this is no time for indecision. The time is here for the great Regulator of the universe to accomplish his battle and trancendent victory.

Chapter 9
Destroyers of the Earth

. . . the time to destroy those
who lay the earth waste.

Revelation 11:18

Civilization in the twentieth century is distinct, all-pervading and pre-eminent in parallelization to the past 6000 years of man's existence. Yet if a comprehensive survey of the globe were to be made, it would be found that in almost every quarter of the globe breeds the climate of self-destruction. Man had explored the earth, scorched it, dredged it, deluged its valleys, violently extracted things from it, concealed things in it, leveled off its mountains, severed its trees, muddied its waters and fouled its air. Wherever man ventures, he infects the sphere with debris and waste.

The word prophet or "prophetess" [meaning "a speaker out front"] is really a misnomer since the death of the apostles. The designation most apropos, and one that conveys a restricted impact, is a "predictor of the future." Predictors of doom have notably increased since the Great War of 1914. Today, and similar to the time of the ancient prophets, there proved to be true and false forecasters. The true forecaster would not be merely a prognosticator, but rather the things that were foretold would come to pass.

Today, and especially since the development of nuclear fisson, a new variety of prophesiers have emerged on the scene. Philosophers, scientists and even politicians have been proclaiming that inevitable disasters are marked for this planet. They say that humanity will eventually suffocate itself into oblivion.

Two years after the first atomic explosion rained genocidal destruction over Japan, scientists fabricated a "doomsday clock" to dramatize the total annihilation of the human race. The clock has become the designated emblem of their publication, "Bulletin of the Atomic Scientists." Should the hands of the clock strike midnight, it would indicate that nuclear war had begun. The scientists think that the atomic overkill capacity of the nations has presented such a monstrous psychodrama that it defies all reasonable doubt. Too often reality is disinvolved or totally neglected, so that there is a danger of people becoming callous to the charades of the ruling class.

Let's surmise, for the sake of argumentation, that the end of the world prophesies are erroneous. Is man ready to risk everything on chance that the earth will survive the machinations of a select few? It is obvious that we are nearing the time when essentially all persons will live in cities. It is also evident that the increasing concerns of most cities are insolvable within the framework of a technological society. The greater number of humanity is distressed, and in all likelihood will have recourse to rebellion with such violence that the inhabitants will be thrown into chaos.

The environment is changing at such an unprecedented velocity that the terminal effect is only dimly recognized. As wastes are heedlessly discharged, cities crowded to suffocation, and farmlands devoured by concrete and asphalt, man seeks to destroy the natural forces that govern life and finds himself in a deteriorating environment with declining resources that might compel the inhabitants to become a transitory happening.

What is happening in our generation is quite dissimilar from what has occurred at any other time. Today, the world is compactly interlaced through sophisticated communication systems, air travel, and socio-economic and political counterchange. Thus, an extreme change on one locality is suddenly felt in another. Authorities admit that the global problems of this system seem certain to grow larger. One explanation why is the unyielding population growth, especially in lands that can least afford it.

People Pollution

One of the most difficult, underhanded, and complex problems to solve is the "population explosion," sometimes referred to as "people pollution." The elapse of time only serves to magnify the problem. Even the most auspicious experts regard the world's swelling population with serious concern because of the inassessibility of food, land, employment and natural resources.

Nearly a decade ago, it was calculated that if all the available land and water were equally dispersed among the population, each person would receive 15 acres of land and approximately 17 acres of water, one-half-mile deep. However, this same person deliberated that by the year 2600, at the average rate of 2 percent a year, the living space would diminish to one square yard for each person.

Well-intentional individuals and organizations have for many years been engrossed in programs to lighten the problems ascribed to population growth. Many solutions have been tested agriculturally, economically and politically. However, as with most remedies that attack the symptom rather than the cause, there has been disappointing results. Most programs have accomplished very little, failed outright or itensified things to the extent that conditions were further impaired.

The cause in part is contributed to a reduction in the death rates as a result of advanced medical care and social conditions. Fewer babies are dying, and more adults are living longer. The root of the problem, however, lies in the manner in which population expands. It does not increase by mere progressive addition, but by submultiple growth. This irrational growth is insidious and misleading. A systems variable can endure through many doubling intervals without seeming to reach a conspicuous measure. But after one or two more duplicating periods, it suddenly seems to become overpowering.

As poor countries extend their agricultural boundaries, they are inclined to spread toward the forests and mountains, thus causing deforestation. Often floods of devastating measure erode the land area. Apparently, even the resources of the seemingly boundless oceans are limited. For example, 21 million tons of fish were taken from the seas in 1950. In 1970, this reached 70 million tons. Then the catch declined, and in 1973, only 65 million tons were harvested. In the past few years, it has seemed that many of the commercial fisheries are being fished too extensively and causing a continuous decline of productivity.

During the time of Jesus, the earth's population grew to an estimated 300 million people. By the early 1800's, it reached one billion and rapidly escalated from that period on. By 1930, or in only a hundred more years, another billion was added, and by 1975, it grew to four billion. Now, the assessed world population stands at more than 4.9 billion inhabitants. If the present rate of expansion were to continue, there would be at least 6,000,000,000 people on earth by the year 2000. Then it would take only eight years for the next thousand million persons to be appended. If that rate were sustained, two hundred years from now there would be almost 200,000,000,000 people on the face of the earth! The entire land area of the globe would become one giant city!

The danger of overcrowding is that it produces abnormal behavior and ultimately, the breakdown of social order. Likewise, it would increase occurrences of mental disorder, alcoholism, drug addiction, crime and suicide.

In international dealings, political and economic pressures would rise immensely with nations compelled to starve to death or invade another's terrain. This would encourage political insecurity and increase the possibility of revolution, antagonism, or the state of war.

As people pollution detonates, the land area that is

usable for farming will actually decrease even faster because cities, habitations, highways, industries and public utilities take away the food harvest. It is apparent that if food and population are not brought into equalization, grave problems will continue to torment the human race. If the population keeps increasing, one day the earth will be more than full. Although it is true that if the wealth of the earth was evenly distributed, there would be more than enough for everyone, but that ideal situation does not exist or ever will in the distant future. It is likely to remain another one of those problems that cannot be solved under the present system of human relations.

The Pollution Virus

Man is losing the struggle against pollution. This menace to life is not in the future—it is immediate. We presently have incidences in which pollution has killed people. Practically in every quarter of the earth, pollution of air, water and land imperils both humans and animals alike. Today, over 800 species and subspecies of animal life are reported to be near extinction. Essentially, there are two causes for the earth's pollution—irrationality and greed on the part of mankind. There has been a sudden increasing amount of evidence so alarming that it cannot be ignored. Man has put himself in such danger that his very existence may be at stake.

Chemical Wastage

"Better Things for Better Living Through Chemistry" was the catchword that announced a new age of progress. However, no one anticipated that the "better things" would create an environmental behemoth. The millions of gallons of chemical waste came with the slogan of "better living." Disastrously, these wastes were often recklessly dumped, thus creating thousands of lethal areas all over the world.

Chemical wastes are now considered the most deplorable water contaminant because they resist natural breaking-down processes and tend to accumulate in animal and human tissue.

In 1980, the U.S. Environmental Protection Agency [EPA] incorporated a program to clean up the country's 400 worst toxic or lethal chemical dump sites. Shortly after that announcement, the agency indexed 144 sites that were considered extremely dangerous to public health, and these sites were to be given the highest priority. Typical among these was one site where chemical leakage became so serious that the community's underground drinking water supply was polluted. Other sites that presented potential dangers included one with 17,000 rusting barrels of toxic wastes and another with 30,000 gallons of poisonous chemicals simply spilled along the roadside.

One country reported that there are some two thousand dumps and over one hundred and eighty thousand chemical lagoons. Half of the population is dependent on that region's underground water supply; therefore, it is fearful that these wastes, plus pesticides from farmlands, are contaminating the water below.

Biologist Barry Commoner, professor at Washington University in St. Louis, Missouri, stated that the environment is being placed under stress "to the point of collapse." He further asserted that the earth is approaching "a crisis which may destroy its suitability as a place for human society." The following is an examination of notable situations that nearly exterminated designated localities:

LOUISIANA—The vast waterways so prevalent in the state of Louisiana are a necessity in the technology of large scale chemical and chemical materials production. Devil's Swamp, a zone that once abounded with a variety of wildlife, was substantially destroyed by the dumping of millions of gallons of deadly chemicals. Almost all the pasturage was contaminated, resulting in 149 cattle deaths. Nearly 550 acres were totally infected. In one residential community near another swamp, people would wake up in the night with a wheezing cough. Dogs who ran near the lethal area would come out with clumps of their hair falling out. In one of the reported 40,000 dump sites in the state, a truck driver was killed because of inhaling toxic fumes while dumping wastes.

LOVE CANAL—The infamous Love Canal episode startled the nation to the point of being indelibly impressed into history. For nearly thirty years the Hooker Chemical Company admittedly dumped 21,800 tons of chemicals within its vicinity. The city of Niagara Falls contributed its portion. The land was sold to the board of education of the city for one dollar with plans for a school and housing development enacted on the site. In time, the ideal neighborhood became a huge chemical graveyard. The choking fumes enveloped the area, and a continuous black mold began seeping through the walls of the schools. The skin began peeling from the children's feet while walking barefooted, and constant migrains were suffered. The inhabitancy experienced birth defects, miscarriages, asthma, cancer, chronic skin rashes and tumors. Suicide and nervous disorders reportedly occurred 27 times more frequently than normal.

TENNESSEE—In Hardeman County, Velsicol Chemical Corporation had buried some 300,000 barrels of poison under three feet of dirt. Banned pesticide 40 times as lethal as DDT, filtered out into the groundwater. Almost all the wells were shut down when residents complained of dizziness, kidney pains, liver disorders, loss of hair, respiratory problems, nausea, limb numbness and even birth defects.

NEW JERSEY—One of the most dangerous spots in the United States is the location where the Chemical Control Corporation, near Elizabeth, stored some 34,000 barrels of leaking chemical waste. The removal of 10,000 of these containing one of the most lethal chemicals produced averted a disaster of monstrous proportions. On April 22, 1980, just 10 miles from the 8.5 million people of New York City, the site exploded into flames. The intense heat rocketed many of the barrels some 200 feet into the air. A huge black cloud formed as fear of a widespread chemical dispersion panicked the population. Residents reportedly have one of the highest cancer rates in the nation.

IOWA—Near Charles City, Salsbury Laboratories dumped countless tons of chemical wastes into a former sand and gravel pit. It was reported that nearly one million cubic feet of deadly arsenic waste was discharged. Contamination had been found in the surrounding groundwater which infected nearby rivers and the wells of the city of Waterloo, some 50 miles away. The area has a higher-than-normal incidence of bladder cancer. The immediate danger, however, was the nearby water aquifer that supplies over 300,000 people.

SEVESCO, ITALY—It was estimated that over 122 pounds of dioxin were released into the air. Four thousand acres of land were contaminated. Thousands of animals died, and crops had to be destroyed. Hundreds of persons developed nausea, blurred vision and severe liver and kidney pains. One thousand acres were evacuated leaving hundreds homeless.

Fossil Fuel

The danger to life is not simply from a widespread dispersion of deadly contaminates. An even more impending danger is that pollution will upset the marvelously complex cycles and balances of the earth's natural state. Today, more than 75 percent of the energy needs of the United States is produced by fossil fuels. This situation is noticed because energy resources are beginning to expire, and the requirements of the rest of the world for these resources is swelling to an even greater extent than this country's. On the average, the world takes from the earth about 2000 million gallons of oil each day. Within ten years if the consumption rate continues, oil use will more than double and intensify as time uncoils. During the next decade, the United States will generate as much electricity as it has generated since its discovery. With the rate of consumption doubling every ten years, all of the earth's fossil fuels will be exhausted in some twenty-five years.

The depletion of energy resources is not itself the crux of the problem. The emission of carbon monoxide, small particulate matter, and other potential pollutants projected over the next two decades are so large that there is a possibility of fundamental changes in the environment. These are produced principally from burning coal and oil in power plants, factories and homes. More terrifying is the established fact that pollution is spreading from one city to another, enshrouding whole sections of the country in a gaseous veil.

Earth's environment can dilute only so much contamination; then it will build up to poisonous levels and load the atmosphere with acid-forming pollutants.

Acid Rain

One of the most serious ecological problems of our generation has been acid rain. In North America, 30 percent of acid rain is caused by nitric oxides—half of these comes from motor vehicle exhausts. The other half comes from burning fossil fuels, mainly coal. These emit sulphur dioxide, which makes up the other 70 percent of acid rain. The annual emission of these gases into the skies is 60 million tons, thus making the atmosphere an interspace garbage dump. These acids also come down in the form of acid hail, sleet, snow, fog and in a dry form.

In high-acid environments, lake waters become unnaturally clear, as plankton and other types of microscopic life expire. The reproduction of aquatic animals is obstructed or even prevented. It generally attacks the gills of fish, literally making them suffocate.

Acid fallout prevents the soil from leaching out essential nutrients such as calcium, magnesium, potassium and sodium. It chokes off the water supply to tree roots and destroys their defenses against disease. In Europe, acid rain is called "an ecological holocaust." In the United States, the Presidential Council on Environmental Quality estimates the damage to buildings and monuments at over 2000 million dollars annually.

As for human health, the evidence of adverse effects of acid rain is inadequate, but still alarming. It has caused diarrhea in babies—and even more frightful—caused bronchitis, emphysema and a strain on the heart and the circulatory system. Only time will reveal the ultimate danger.

Pesticides

Much of the world's food is lost each year to pests. Thus in 1979 alone, 6.4 billion pounds of pesticides were produced—well over a pound for every person on earth. Many of these chemicals, some of which do not break down, cling to vegetables and fruits or enter the food chain where they are stored in the meat that is consumed. So virtually everyone on earth has in his body an unknown amount of these pollutants.

Hexachlorobenzene

Researchers have detected hexachlorobenzene [HCB] in the atmosphere of the most remote area of the Pacific Ocean. Chances are there isn't any place on earth you can go without finding the chemical. The relative constancy of the compound between sites suggests that HCB is very stable and may remain in the atmosphere a long time. It has been found to cause cancer in laboratory animals and is a by-product of more than a dozen manufacturing processes, including rubber.

Nuclear Power

There are more than one hundred and thirty nuclear power plants in operation in the United States. About 25 percent of the nation's electricity is generated by these facilities. Likewise, other nations are using nuclear energy to produce electricity. There is a prodigious power within the atom, so it is reasonable that people would be concerned about the safety of splitting the atom and the harnessing of such energy. Can the radioactivity that is produced harm man?

As with most exploits of mankind, there are conflicting opinions. The Atomic Energy Commission and the electric industry would have the populus believe that atomic energy is unthreatening. One television commercial illustrated a burning match and said in effect—a nuclear power plant emits less pollution than this match. However, certain news reports may cause one to doubt the soundness in those claims.

Ironically, a Minnesota nuclear plant was accorded an operating license by the Commission that would allow a stack release of 41,800 curies a day in radioactive emission. Some atomic scientists fearfully asserted that radioactive emissions greater than 860 curies posed a threat to public health. Scientists John W. Gofman and Arthur R. Tamplin said they "believed that the public is being deceived by a clever, well-financed propaganda campaign of delusion about clean, cheap, safe nuclear power."

Obversely to popular assumption, electric power is not generated directly from the splitting of atoms within the nuclear factory. Rather, fission within the reactor simply produces a source of heat. Therefore, it replaces the furnace of a conventional plant. Heat from the reactor boils water and produces steam. The steam turns a turbine, and the turbine, in turn, drives a generator to produce energy.

The nuclear reactor's tremendous heat is produced in long, slender, metal-clad fuel rods. These are filled with small pellets of uranium dioxide which give each rod the potential energy of 6,000 tons of coal. In a large reactor, there may be some 40,000 fuel rods that contain over one hundred tons of uranium pellets. That is more uranium than is found in over one hundred atomic bombs. The reactor's heat is produced by splitting the atoms of the uranium isotope U-235. In order to control the rate of the fission process, long control rods that absorb flying neutrons are inserted into the reactor core. Thus, the rate of fission is controlled by the positioning in the core of these rods.

One billion uranium atoms are split in the reactor every second. They, in turn, form smaller atoms of other elements that are radioactive. In one year, a large reactor can produce as much long-persisting radioactivity as would be emitted in the explosion of a thousand Hiroshima bombs. As long as the terrifying amount of radioactivity stays within the fuel rods, there is no danger. But does all remain there?

Radioactivity is emitted into the air through the plant's stack. It also enters into the water used in the reactor and is thus released into a river or lake. Gaseous atoms also leak out through imperfections in the metal casings of the fuel rods. Even if no radiation falls directly on humans within the immediate vicinity, still there is a grave danger to those living many miles away. And again, radioactivity can become concentrated in food supplies. It may settle on grass and be eaten by cows, then become contracted in their milk. Dr. Ernest J. Sternglass, a professor of radiation physics at the University of Pittsburgh Medical School, indicated that already nuclear power plants are responsible for infant deaths. He offers data that shows an excess of infant deaths in areas near nuclear reactors.

The danger also exists for accidents due to human miscalculations or equipment defection. Many fear that in the event of an earthquake the plant can be broken open with large amounts of radioactive debris scattered by the winds. Already, large amounts have been discharged due to accidents at nuclear facilities.

Space does not permit an extensive study on the subject. The disposal of radioactive wastes has only been hinted at, and the danger of thermal or heat pollution has only been touched upon as to its effects on the reduced oxygen content of the globe's rivers and lakes. The most catastrophic danger would be if a third world war plagued the planet where reactor damage would be par for the course.

It is obvious that nuclear power is not as safe as industry promoted advertisements might lead persons to believe. The late Supreme Court Justice Hugo Black called this means of generation "the most awesome, the most deadly, the most dangerous process that man has ever conceived."

Militarization

Mankind has entered into an inexperienced age of warfare with awesome means of mass destruction. In the past, general wars always occurred when a great power tried to compensate for economic and political decline by resorting to decisive military means. However, trying to solve economic problems with military buildups today would mean total annihilation.

What is especially significant about the coming decade is not merely the inevitable spread of atomic weapons, but the nations to which these weapons will likely spread. It is improbable that nuclear proliferation can be stopped. There is virtually too much plutonium available from which bombs can be made, and the know-how to make bombs is readily accessible. Thus far, a total of 110,000 kilograms of plutonium in an unprocessed state has been amassed from civilian nuclear reactors. It only takes a few kilograms to make a bomb like the one that destroyed Nagasaki.

World leaders have perceived a conflict between the superpowers is inevitable before the end of this century. One should never forget this reality. Not for thirty years has political tension reached so dangerous a point as it has today. Not in all this time has there been such a great degree of distortion, skepticism, perplexity, and mere military dismay.

The list of doomsday weapons is endless, despite disarmament talks and peace agreements. Tens of thousands of bombs equivalent to 60 million tons of TNT are stockpiled in many arsenals. The United States alone has enough atomic warheads to destroy every man, woman and child on earth 12 times over. But the firepower is only one frightening development.

Many may still feel somewhat protected knowing they are thousands of miles from an unfriendly nation. Today, however, there are systems primed to deliver atomic warheads whose accuracy defies imagination. Missiles conveying up to eight distinct atomic warheads are capable of traveling 6,000 miles and hitting the target within 492 yards. Clearly, no one on earth can really feel secure.

To reinforce the overkill tactics, some nations have armed themselves with chemical and biological weapons. New death sprays are being manufactured with the most minute droplets being able to cause heart attacks. The inducement to strike first will increase dangerously, and the risk of nuclear war by misjudgment, accident or unsoundness of mind will undoubtedly increase. Consider other weapons of destruction.

The most fatal of the agents, especially nerve gas, is beyond expectation. A drop of tabun or soman, the size of a pinhead on the arm, will kill a person in three to six minutes. Because these chemicals or biological agents are available in great quantities, it can be directed against livestock or crops.

Between 1963 and 1978, a total of 1,536 satellites serving military purposes were launched into space. Such satellites are used for reconnaissance, early warning systems, and communication, and are especially important for navigation. Researchers believe that soon, by means of a satellite-based navigation system, it will be possible to guide a weapon anywhere on earth to within 33 feet of its target.

In addition to these military achievements, men are still searching for new ways of mass destruction. Constant attention is being given to the manipulation of geophysical or environmental forces for hostile purposes. It includes tampering with the electrical properties of the ionosphere or troposphere to disrupt enemy communications, radar systems, navigation and missile-guidance systems. Additionally, techniques for initiating hurricanes or cyclones, or for redirecting natural ones, would make an immense destructive force available to the military. It is even surmised that there is the possibility of controlling cloud-to-ground lightening for attacks.

The layer of ozone within the lower stratosphere that shields the inhabitants from harmful amounts of ultraviolet radiation is also viewed as a potential weapon. The chemical element bromine appears to be so effective at ozone depletion that it could be used as a weapon. If injected into the stratosphere, it would purge the ozone, permitting ultraviolet radiation to reach the ground with sufficient intensity to destroy crops and incapacitate the inhabitants.

Even the land could be used against an enemy. It might be possible to trigger an earthquake, induce a sleeping volcano situated in enemy territory, or disrupt landforms to cause avalanches or landslides.

Devastating wildfires can be initiated by military action and by the employment of highly efficient delayed-action incendiary devices and scattered antipersonnel mines. A wildfire could be made virtually impossible to extinguish.

Rainmaking is already used in modern warfare. In the Indochina war, aircraft seeded the clouds with such agents as silver iodide and lead iodide. The resultant rains ruined enemy lines of communication, hampered enemy offensives, aided bombing missions and created generally disruptive floods.

Never before have nations been in a position to destroy the very basis of the continued existence of other nations; never before has the destructive capacity of weapons been so immediate, complete and universal; never before has mankind been faced with the real danger of self-extinction.

The act of destroying the earth is not the way man was commanded to subdue it. Logically, education began with the first of human life that was agreeable to fixed principles. They were not to decide within themselves their own course of action (Jeremiah 10:23). No matter how many billions of years the earth might have reeled about the universe, no matter how many aeons of time the Creator spent in preparing its life processes, the time arrived when he turned over its preservation to man. Today, however, man has taken hold of such power with a destructive intent.

Men and nations are found guilty before earth's Owner and Supreme Judge. They intentionally with violent endeavor hang the endangerment of nuclear destruction over the planet. It is another situation that, while each side regards the population of the other side as the innocent victims of unjust government, each intends to punish the other government even if it means annihilating the already suffering and oppressed population.

God will not tolerate earth's demise. He will intervene.

You may hear some jeer at the relevance of Revelation where it warns "to bring to ruin those ruining the earth," but let man challenge the warning. Let him put matters to the test. But just as men cannot survive their ruination of the earth, neither can they survive the demarcating war of Armageddon.

Chapter 10
Spirits of Antipathy

. . . in time past ye walked
according to the prince of
the power of the air.

Ephesians 2:2

The spread of psychic phenomena already has a greater control over human society than most people realize. Whether superstitious or not, the masses have a peculiar fascination for the occult, for powers of a hidden source, for happenings of a supernatural kind. That spiritualists receive messages and induce energy from the unknown cannot be questioned. The groundwork for such a spread of spiritualism was laid millenniums ago. The spirtualists seem to produce the proof of their belief in their actual experiences and in the phenomena they are able to demonstrate. Psychic science calls it *Immortalism*; however, in truth and practice it is *demonism*. It is this power exercised over the human mind that will eventually destroy society.

Spiritualism is about four thousand years old, but it had its origin in America in 1848. It was then certain rappings in the house of one Mr. Fox at Hideville, New York, were heard. The rappings could not be accounted for, and it was said that communications could be held with the spirit of the departed. These raps were arranged in a sort of alphabetical order for the purpose of the supposed communications and were supplemented by the motion of articles of furniture about the room. Then musical instruments were said to sail about the room and utter unearthly melodies; sentences were written by unseen hands; shadowy forms were seen in the darkness; light touches were felt;

and, lastly, the complete embodiment of a spirit was recognized by relatives.

The believers in these manifestations increased very rapidly, and many converts were made in England. In the United States, it was said that at one time no fewer than 30,000 spirit mediums were practicing.

The general conclusion drawn respecting the nature and form of these demonic spirits seems to be that they are embodied in some pure corporeal substance of a highly attenuated kind which is not subject to the ordinary laws of matter. Yet these demonic spirits appear to have some bodily form that enables them to apply force to physical objects and perform actions such as writing and producing sounds. It is often claimed that these demonic spirits sometime appear as a translucent materialized specter. Since the power to materialize fleshly bodies was taken from them just prior to the flood of Noah's day, the material or ectoplasm was evidently borrowed from the subject or medium.

The nearest thing to an apparition that was within their control was the power to invade the bodies of men who were already living. These demonic spirits could possess and drive to satisfy their sadistic and unnatural desires through the bodies of men. Religion has not advanced enough in knowledge, purity, and brotherly love to create a defense against the powers of the occult. An appeal to the spiritualistic or spiritistic has become the fashion for the entire world and is claimed by many to be an adjunct to the Christian religion.

Demonic Activity

The resurgence of witchcraft, voodooism, spiritualism, divination and other forms of demonism in these times is truly a fulfillment of the "last days." The invisible wicked forces are aware of their impending destruction and therefore create violence and corruption throughout the inhabited earth. In order to identify these forces and the diabolic manipulation they employ, it would be advantageous to examine their abilities, pleasures and unsavory sphere of influence these forces hold over the masses.

It can be assumed from their original residence in heaven that these forces possess knowledge far beyond our present conception. They are superior to man in strength, and their abilities transcend the power of human language.

In the account of the two men that were demon-possessed, a rather interesting situation transpired:

> "When he got to the other side, into the country of the Gadarenes, there met him two demon-possessed men coming out from among the memorial tombs, unusually fierce, so nobody had the courage to pass by on that road. And, look! they screamed, saying: What have we to do with you, Son of God? Did you come here to torment us before the appointed time?' But a long way off from them a herd of swine was at pasture. So the demons began to entreat him saying: If you expel us, send us forth into the herd of swine' " (Matthew 8:28-31).

The demons did not want to confront the Son of God and fearfully made an early reference to their thousand year imprisonment. They entreated Jesus to "send them forth into the herd of swine." This request exhibits much detail for the inquirer. It would show the observers, in a forceful manner, the harm that could befall creatures of flesh that allowed themselves to become possessed. More importantly, it demonstrated Jesus' power over the demons and their diabolical control over those of the flesh.

The appeal from the demons was for quite another reason. It was possible that they derived a pleasurable excitement in some sadistic way. To invade some fleshly body was not natural for the spirit creatures; however, it is discernable that on occasions they desired to do so.

A relevant example of this distortion presented itself prior to the flood of Noah's day. Rebellious spirit creatures enleagued themselves with Satan and materialized in human form to cohabit with fleshly women. It was to be a longevous relationship and permitted them to delight in practices that were not of a spiritual nature. It amounted to an unnatural proximity and resulted in an offspring of sadistic hybrids (Genesis 6:1-4). They were eventually forced to return to spirit form for their own preservation.

It was a kind of perversion that prepossessed some degenerate men who sank to sodomy and to other men rather than women for intercourse. So the demons, when they could not reside in the man, wanted to be allowed to enter the swine. It gave them the opportunity to vent their sadistic desires by ganging up on men, since many possessed one person.

Sadistic men have always derived morbid thrills for perverted and abnormal sex crimes and violence (Genesis 19:4-11). There is no reason to conclude that demon possession cannot be forced upon men today. If the spiritual weakness of the masses is evident, they present themselves surmountable for assaults and inducement.

The incident involving King Saul gave further discursive reasoning to the danger confronting men and the uncanny abilities of the demons. Saul became repulsive to God, therefore severing his relationship and divine directions that were needed to pursue his incumbency. When the Philistines waged war against him, he was compelled to confer with a spirit medium. He requested that she bring back the dead prophet Samuel for consultation:

"At this the woman said: 'Whom shall I bring up for you?' To this he said: 'Bring up Samuel for me. . . . ' But the king said to her: 'Do not be afraid, but what did you see?' And the woman went on to say to Saul: 'A god I saw coming up out of the earth.' At once he said to her: 'What is his form?' to

210

which she said: 'It is an old man coming up, and he has himself covered with a sleeveless coat.' At that Saul recognized that it was Samuel and he proceeded to bow low with his face to the earth and to prostrate himself. And Samuel began to say to Saul: 'Why have you disturbed me by having me brought up?' " (1 Samuel 28:11- 15).

Since the dead is linked with silence [See Psalm 115:17], and God's favor was withdrawn from Saul, it is conceivable that it was not Samuel. It was evident that the act of consulting a spirit medium constituted a violation of God's law (Leviticus 20:6, 27). Saul himself acknowledged that "God himself has departed from me and has answered me no more." It becomes clear that the manifestation was a deception conspired by invisible wicked forces. Being intelligent creatures of a spiritual nature, they could very well impersonate the dead to feed their fiendish appetite. The identical source of illusion is exhibited by spiritualists today.

An experience involving a Roman official, Sergius Paulus, who was proconsul of Cyprus, sheds further light in this spiritual pretext. The account indicates that he was an "intelligent man" and was searching for the truth. He asked the apostle Paul to reveal the Creator to him and the newly established Christianity. However, a sorcerer [diviner] named Elymas began resisting Paul. Paul, in turn, came face to face with him and exposed the source of his occult powers. He said, "O man full of every sort of fraud and every sort of villainy, you son of the Devil, you enemy of everything righteous, will you not quit distorting the right ways of God?" (Acts 13:6-10).

The same origin of involvement was evident in fortune-telling at the time Paul was preparing his missionary assignment into Europe. A girl was possessed with a demon of divination, and her masters were realizing a considerable profit from her feats of making predictions. She persistently implored Paul to release her from this curse. Finally Paul got tired of it and turned and said to the spirit, "I order you in the name of Jesus Christ to come out of her" (Acts 16:18). She then lost her fortune-telling ability, thus disclosing the obscene power behind this diabolical activity.

Bible history records that many sons of God [angels] chose independence from their Creator. They have tremendous powers and influence over the minds and lives of vulnerable persons, even the ability to possess humans or animals and use inanimate objects for their deceptive intentions.

Present-day Divination

Spiritistic practices are perceivably on the increase, fluctuating in degree and form from place to place. If the demon activity is more existent in certain areas, the more harrassment and demonic afflictions are manifested.

The assault by wicked forces can take on many guises. *From actual cases*, we know there may be a slap to the face, or a body blow, a throwing of one about, bodily illness or pain [Compare Matthew 12:22; Mark 1:26; 9:17, 18, 25; Luke 11:14]. One may be annoyed while trying to sleep due to the pervasion of abnormal noises. There may a pulling of bed covers, a shaking of the bed, an apparition such as a face or a pair of impaling eyes. Often a voice is heard that harasses and terrorizes. But how does one become involved to come under demonic influence? By dabbling in practices associated with spiritism.

Astrology

Astrology is a form of divination, therefore, it can involve one in spiritism. Diabolical forces can manipulate circumstances so that it may sometimes appear that astrology is a reliable means of forecasting events. In going after the illusionary practice, one could be brought under the jurisdiction of the devil. Paul, in his first letter to Timothy, warned that those living in our day would be "paying attention to misleading inspired utterances and teachings of demons." So the growing popular interest in spiritism or the occult arts is understandable.

Rich and poor alike read their horoscope daily. In the United States, it has been surmised that some 15 million people religiously follow astrology, and about fifty million more have some contact with it.

In ancient times, the astrologers concluded that the heavenly movements would influence the character of man. This was perceived because they thought the earth was the center of the universe. The zodiac was divided into twelve equal parts of 30° each called the "signs of the zodiac." Eventually, each sign received the name of the constellation that occupied the designated position. As with many practices adopted by an unsteady civilization, the history of astrology can be traced back to ancient Babylonia in its earliest phase.

Fortune-Telling

Throughout the world, fortune-tellers enjoy a thriving business. Hundreds of millions of dollars are paid annually to people who profess to have special ability to foretell the future. Some individuals visit a fortune-teller every day and will not make a decision without such a consultation.

Fortune-telling entails the predicting of one's fortune or future by professed observable signs or indications construed by amateur or professional diviners. Therefore, it is a form of divination or a method of securing knowledge of the unknown by supernatural means. It could be ventured by methods such as cartomacy [with cards], chiromancy [palmistry], or crystallomancy [with a crystal ball]. Many methods are performed by looking for and interpreting omens or signs that are inferred to foreshadow future events. Astrology carries the same connotation as it utilizes the sun, moon, stars and planets, as well as other means of divination.

In Palmistry, the lines and other characteristics of the palm are spoken of as having "mounts" named after the seven planets known to ancient astrologers. The Tarot cards include twenty-two Tarots [trumps] and fifty-six numeral cards. They are divided into four suits with each suit and each card given a specific meaning. The Tarot readers base their interpretation upon the structure of the universe, chiefly the solar system as symbolized by the Holy Cabala. The Cabala divides up the universe into three elements [fire, air and water], seven planets, and the twelve signs of the zodiac. It conjures up strange power and becomes a playground for the supernatural influence beyond the realm of human comprehension.

Ouija Board

Many of those who utilize the board claim they can communicate with the other world. Even prominent political leaders have undeniably used it for similar reasons. Just what is the ouija board? Is it merely an innocent amusement? Or is it really a means of communicating with spirits of the other world?

The ouija board was placed on the market in the 1890's by a Baltimore manufacturer. The name was extracted from the German and French words for "yes." The board contains the words "Yes," "No," "Goodbye," the letters of the alphabet, and the numbers one through nine and zero. Atop this sits a heart shaped device mounted on three felt-tipped legs. When consultants place their hands on this, a force causes it to move about the board, spelling out words and sentences that can provide information not previously known to the persons using the board. Obviously, in many cases, there is an intelligently directed force at work. Isaiah 1:13 emphatically states, "I cannot put up with the use of uncanny power [or a'wen] along with the solemn assembly." The Hebrew word "a'wen" denotes strength but chiefly false strength, a magic power; therefore, it involves witchcraft and magic arts. There have been many frightening experiences with this source of uncanny power. It is quite clear that experimenting with the Ouija board could have only a detrimental effect on one.

Hypnotism

Hypnosis has been shrouded in mystery for many centuries. It was once used by pagan priests and charlatans. Today it is used by psychiatrists, dentists, clergymen and others. It has been lauded as an aid for many endeavors in medicine and used as a means to cure psychosomatic disorders. Some practitioners have been driven insane. It was used to coerce the subject to steal; it compelled the subject to pick up rattlesnakes, and even to throw sulphuric acid into a man's face. Those *actual cases* make hypnosis a compelling factor to force persons to commit crimes or involuntary immoral acts. The very possibility of danger merits serious consideration.

This controlling influence is apparently a human, but it puts its victim under a spell. It can lead a hypnotized person to produce spiritualistic phenomena. In hypnotism, some people have developed an E.S.P. faculty and were able to revert to psychic powers.

No human knows exactly how hypnotism works, therefore, one should not ignore its background. An encyclopedia of occultism declares that "its history is inextricably interwoven with occultism; and, even today, much hypnotic phenomena is classed as spiritualistic." It is merely the reproduction of the practice of ancient magic produced by the same methods employed by pagan magicians, sorcerers, wizards and necromancers. Even if hypnosis had no occult associations, true Christians would want to shun it because it requires one to completely surrender his will to another.

Extrasensory Perception

Extrasensory perception [ESP] is the faculty of certain persons to acquire knowledge of things without using the recognized senses of sight, smell, taste, hearing and touch. It includes telepathy, familiarization with another person's thoughts, clairvoyance, the consciousness of events, objects or individuals without using the normal senses; psychokinesis, the ability to control objects by focalization; and precognition, perception of the future. Since miraculous powers in the Bible were to glorify God and promote true worship, it is only logical to conclude that ESP, along with other supernatural manifestations, is not a product of truth.

Any means that is used to discover hidden knowledge is another form of divination. An encyclopedia of occultism asserts that "clairvoyance [form of ESP] remains to the present day a prominent feature of the spiritualistic seance." Serious harm has resulted to many who become involved with this diabolical deception. In reality, ESP can cause people to look to evil forces rather than the true source of light for guidance.

Dungeons and Dragons

"Dungeons and Dragons" is a popular game that creates a mythological world of violence. Players assume the identity of characters who become part of a world controlled by the Dungeon Master. Imaginary surroundings are mapped out by the players who question the Dungeon Master. He, in turn, assumes the role of any monster or medley of characters the players may encounter. He also determines their fate with the aid of specially shaped dice. As the players pursue a latent treasure, the Dungeon Master attempts to kill them by means of his monsters.

This is typical of most games that have invaded the teenage marketplace today. There is hardly a game in which the players do not indulge in murder, torture, rape, arson or

216

robbery. The player on many occasions becomes so absorbed into the nature of the character that he becomes a part of the fantastical dilemma. Many such superego players, after succumbing to defeat and death, actually suffer psychic shock and may go into depression.

The game teaches greed, materialism, violence, polytheism and demonism. Included in the game are magic users such as mediums, seers, conjurers, goblins, hellhounds, hobgoblins, ogres, skeletons, specters, vampires and zombies. As the play progresses into the advanced level, demonism becomes more prevalent. "Dungeons and Dragons" pervades the structure of a satanic order, and characters are expected to dedicate themselves to a mythological god.

Pharmakeia

Drugs have unquestionably become a major contention, especially since they have spread into colleges, high schools and lower grade levels. They have been marketed as a way to get relief from the pressures of the world. To the many that advocate their use, they become "a way to get closer to God." "They give instant paradise." "They give one the sense of awareness" or "instant self-analysis."

Whom does the use of drugs really help one to approach? Isn't it the powers of darkness? The realistic approach to drugs is that they have all the advantages of death without its permanence. Statistics have indicated that a shocking 62 percent of drug abusers were enticed to the deadly danger of spiritism, demon practices and worship, and obsession. In Galatians 5:19-21, the "works of the flesh" are listed. Is it possible that the use of drugs can lead to all of them? As with spiritism, drug use promotes the perverted and debased practices of demonomancy.

Demonic activity is evident in almost every facet of life today. Children are being entertained by ghoulish or demonic villains on television and in illustrative comic books. Some children find it difficult to separate the imaginary from reality. Movies cater to the dangerous fascination of exacting violence and demonistic debauchery. Modern music is categorized into five basic themes: sex, drugs, violence, occult, and rebellion. Some music groups are admittedly deeply involved in the occult, and the lyrics often appear to promote these themes. The ultimate result is the suppression of all mental tendencies, conscious or latent.

Fantasy and the supernatural have an obsessing charm to an increasing number of persons. They have matured in a world that is morally and spiritually impoverished. Religion has done little to satisfy and prepare the masses for demonic assault. Politicians have often been deplorable examples and have left their followers frustrated. Popular philosophies have really diminished a faith in a Supreme Being. Hence, it is no wonder that many youths experiment with everything from absurd religious cults and practices to hallucinating drugs. And such practices prosper because so many people actually seem to experience something personally, a phenomenon that is completely void in a problematic society.

Diabolical Seduction

Both religion and science are disunited as to whether transcendental happenings actually occur. Some believe that alleged occult experiences are merely indications of mental disorders or errors in reporting. Others assert that, rather than being proof of the supernatural, such experiences show that mankind itself may have hidden psychic powers still ascertained by technics. However, occultists maintain that there is a spirit realm at work through these unnatural manifestations.

Those who are implicated in occult formalities themselves recognize that there is a danger involved. One reason for this is that using the Ouija board, holding séances or practicing ESP are summonings to malicious spirits with the possibility of an unlimited possession. No matter how counteractive and different the occult practices are, the combined purpose is to allure human beings away from true Christianity and cause them to rely entirely upon their own volition.

The diabolic profoundness behind this scheme is evident. People are fascinated by unheard-of, seemingly supernatural phenomena. The assortment of occult practices appeals to dissimilar types of people. Some subject themselves directly to Satan through devil worship, voodoo, witchcraft and so forth. Others are deceived by innocently dabbling in astrology or spiritualism. Those with a scientific mind often become intrigued with psychic powers such as ESP or clairvoyance. There is a clique for almost everyone.

History testifies that almost all early peoples were deeply engrossed in occultism. Yet just one nation is known to have had a religion that avoided the occult—the ancient Hebrews of the Bible. In unmistakable terms, God specified the practices that they were to avoid:

> "There must never be anyone among you who makes his son or daughter pass through fire, who practices divination, who is a soothsayer, auger or sorcerer, who uses charms, consults ghosts or spirits, or calls up the dead. For the man who does these things is detestable to Yahweh your God; it is because of these detestable practices that Yahweh your God is driving these nations before you" (Deuteronomy 18:10-12).

All forms of divination, whether through interpretation of omens or by some other use of psychic powers, are covered by that prohibition.

Sadistic Encounters

The origin of evil and the fall of Satan from heaven is indistinctly known to mankind. Although people are left greatly in obscurity as to his fall, one is not ignorant to his works. Temptations are real, and to many who were subjugated to unseen intruders, the frightful experience will undoubtedly remain with them. Now please consider several of the more notable encounters as reported by reliable sources.

One of the most convincing cases to have come to the attention of parapsychologist J. B. Rhine, was a 14-year-old boy, often assaulted in the bedroom. *The Philadelphia News* reported that when the boy was taken to a minister's house to sleep, the bed shook so violently that he had to get up and try to sleep in a heavy armchair. While the clergyman stood over him, the chair tilted to one side and fell over, throwing the boy to the floor. The minister tried the same posture in the chair and could not even tilt it due to the weighty construction.

In another case in Runcorn, Cheshire, England, the "Daily Colonist" of Victoria, Canada asserted that visible hands kept throwing a boy out of bed at night. The Methodist cleric W. H. Stevens who witnessed the incident, reported that the spirit hurled a Bible at him when he attempted to help the child.

Many times the assaults are of such a nature that it is utterly impossible to attribute them to dreams. *The London Daily Mail* tells an episode of a man and wife at Epsom where the wife experiences bedroom disturbances. Something was tugging at her shoulders and eventually dragged her towards the window of the room. She cried for help, and her husband grabbed her legs. But whatever it was had great strength, even to the point of dragging her husband. Suddenly, they said, it seemed to lose its power and released her.

New Zealand's *Auckland Star* reported that while twelve policemen and twenty civilians searched an area for unseen distrubances, a guest house at Brooklyn was peppered with stones for seven and a half hours. Neither radar nor dogs helped to solve the mystery.

The *Panama City Herald* told of an 18-year-old girl who was harassed by spirits. While in the presence of city officials and a doctor, she was attacked, and her hand was badly bitten.

The *Singapore Sunday Times* wrote of unseen attacks on children. The spirit was said to have attacked young girls and children, sometimes stripping them naked and often causing them to groan in agony.

When the motion picture about demon possession [Exorcist II] was shown on American television, a mother and her 4-year-old daughter in Wichita Falls, Texas, reportedly watched it together. One scene depicted cutting out of the girl's heart to get rid of a demon. The little Texas girl was later found murdered in the same fashion. Her mother was charged with the homocide although she had no recollection of her crime.

From all over the world come reports of harmful assaults from the unknown. They number in the thousands and consist not only of demon assaults, but also of angry conversations between attempting exorcists and the wicked spirits. These voices many times have induced the recipient to violence, murder and even suicide.

Religious Seduction

How are we to view the works of healing, speaking in tongues, exorcism, and so forth, found within many denominations of Christendom? Does this not indicate that God is manifesting his power to defeat the onslaught of demon activity? Jesus comtemplated this question and delivered a surprising reply:

"Be on the watch for the false prophets that come to you in sheep's covering, but inside they are ravenous wolves. By their fruits you will recognize them. . . . Not everyone saying to me, 'Lord, Lord,' will enter the kingdom of the heavens, but the one

221

doing the will of my Father. . . . Many will say to me in that day, 'Lord, Lord, did we not prophesy in your name, and expel demons in your name, and perform many powerful works in your name?' And yet then I will confess to them: 'I never knew you! Get away from me, you workers of lawlessness' " (Matthew 7:15-23).

It is evident that those counterfeit Christians who used the name of Christ are as detestable to God as occultists were among the Hebrew nation. The identical authoritative source was behind both occurrences. Do not presuppose that all miraculous works performed in the name of Christianity is authentically from God. "Test the inspired expression to see whether they originate with God" (I John 4:1). Paul, in his second letter to the Thessalonica congregation, contrasted the "love of the truth" with "deceptive signs" when he warned:

"But the lawless one's presence is according to the operation of Satan with every powerful work and lying signs and portents and with every unrighteous deception for those who are perishing, as a retribution because they did not accept the love of the truth that they might be saved" (2 Thessalonians 2:9, 10).

Since the release of the productions, "The Exorcist I and II," a wave of exorcism frenzy has been generated throughout the United States. The occult is becoming so popular in England that the Anglican Church had appointed exorcists in every region of the country to cope with resultant problems. The capability of an individual to exorcise, or expel demons does not necessarily indicate that God backs up the men who profess to have such powers. Professed Christians as well as non-Christians claim success at this practice. In one's examination, remember, God does not work against himself by sustaining opposing factions. Also, the very procedure employed by most so-called exorcists show that they do not originate with God. Jesus could cast out the spirits *with a word,* simply commanding them, and they obeyed. Exorcists today utilize ritualistic, magical formulas citing certain words or phrases that are assumed to possess the power to exorcise. The Roman Catholic formula for exorcism, found in the *Rituale Romanum,* can take *several hours* to recite and uses religious relics and other superstitious religious paraphernalia.

The more science explores the unknown, the more it is faced with the evidences of an occult power of invisible forces bringing about supernatural acts and happenings among men.

It should be noted that the invisible demon spirits have a strong desire to be in close association with humans. They are contented to forsake their heavenly position for the pleasure of living in the state of fornication. The Scriptures confirm that although they are constrained from such physical contact, they have not altered their desires. They seek every means within their power to be in touch with humans and to dominate them. Jesus asserted, ". . . when an evil spirit comes out of man, it goes through arid places seeking rest and does not find it. Then it says, I will return to the house I left. When it arrives, it finds the house unoccupied, swept clean and put in order. Then it goes and takes with it seven other spirits more wicked than itself, and they go in and live there. And the final condition of that man is worse than the first. That is how it will be with this wicked generation" (Matthew 12:43-45).

Remember, curiosity can lead to one coming under demonic control. It is wise to shun all forms of divination and exert oneself to resist being deceived by these wicked forces. Since God's view has not changed, the culmination of all things is inevitable. Uncontrollable forces seem to be shaping a catastrophic future for mankind. It has caused many to feel there must be greater powers than allowed by purely materialistic thinking. The march of all the worldly nations to the greatest and most destructive war in all human history is unquestionably being conducted under demon influence. Though by no means has everything been told, early man did not sentimentalize over unseen phenomenal powers, did not worship them as beautiful, did not care much for them one way or another until they forced themselves upon his attention by becoming pertinent to his life and needs. However, when this happened he took steps at once to bring himself into an adulterous relationship with them.

Chapter 11
The Day the Lion Roars

. . . Look! the Lion that is of
the tribe of Judah, the root
of David, has conquered.

Revelation 5:5

"Armageddon" is a Biblical expression, and in the last
book of the Bible, it is mentioned only once. However, that
prophetic term has made such a strong impression upon the
minds of the populus, it has become almost a household
word.

The opinions have been quite diversified as to the
nature, location, participants, time and effect of this final
war. Some presume that it pertains to events in an earlier
time of history. Many politicians have utilized it when they
considered the world to be in a crisis, whether by war,
natural disasters or other uncontrollable disturbances. Others infer that Armageddon is a perpetual struggle amid the
forces of good and evil. Generally, it has been viewed by
mankind as a final or nuclear war to be fought between
communism and the western democratic bloc of nations. In
his book, *The Late Great Planet Earth*, the author adds to
this latter illusion by designating the location to be the
literal Mount of Megiddo.

To hold to these opinions, however, is to grossly misin-
terpret both the nature and magnitude of Armageddon. It
would be a serious mistake to dismiss the great war lightly
because of misapplied prophecies as were supposed. The
region of Megiddo could not logically maintain all "the
kings of the earth and their armies." Armageddon will be
greater than any nuclear war fought on a global or even an

225

interspacial scale. It will be a war among gods and will be universal in measure.

Armageddon

Men, by means of their peace talks, concordats, compacts, leagues and strategies cannot avoid the confrontation. Since the Bible is the source of the term, it is appropriate that we examine the master battle projection and the forces involved. Prophetic meanings described in previous chapters of this book are bracketed to facilitate a better understanding:

> "And the sixth one poured out his bowl upon the great river Euphrates [or Babylonian organized religion] and its waters were dried up [lack of support from peoples and nations], that the way might be prepared for the kings [Yahweh and his Christ] from the rising of the sun. And I saw three unclean inspired expressions [propaganda] like frogs come out of the mouth of the dragon [Satan] and out of the mouth of the wild beast [United Nations] and out of the mouth of the false prophet [Anglo-American World Power]. They are, in fact, expressions inspired by demons and perform signs, and they go forth to the kings of the entire inhabited earth, to gather them together to the war of the great day of God, the Almighty. . . . And they gathered them together in the place that is called in Hebrew Har-Magedon." (Revelation 16:12-16).

Actually, the name "Har-Magedon" does not refer to a geographical location as generally reasoned. In fact, the place is nonexistent on any geographical map of the world. Armageddon is a Greek transliteration, or equivalent of the Hebrew expression, and is unseverable with the "war of the great day of God the Almighty." This disregards its relevance to mental struggles, bygone history, political battles or a nuclear holocaust between the king of the north and the king of the south.

Observe carefully that the prophetic vision indicated that the armed nations were being gathered together for war. This assembling of troops is not from the functioning of the Holy Spirit, but rather through certain propaganda doctrine or teaching of "unclean expressions inspired by demons." The worldly political and religious elements were liable, and this hard fact in itself is reason enough why war with God is inevitable. Since it is the war of God the Almighty it would also denote an issue regarding His sovereignty as well as the involvement of opposing kingdoms. Make no mistake, the Creator who provided the sun, moon, stars, and the revolution of the earth for man's calculations, has an appointed time for this final decision.

The reality of a conflict would signify opposing sides. According to Revelation 19:11, 14, a vast army of invisible spirit forces, led by the rider on the white horse, Jesus Christ, will rally on God's side. The use of heavenly armies, numbering 200,000,000 on one occasion, shows the huge invisible forces at God's command (Revelation 9:16).

Amassed in opposition are Satan and his demonic hosts, the invisible enemy. How many cohorts Satan has is not recorded; however, their total number can by no means be insignificant. The demonic forces are potent as can be visualized from the fact that *one of them* once restrained an angel for twenty-one days, until the archangel Michael came to end the struggle (Daniel 10:13, 21).

Likewise, a visible earthly component stands adverse to God. Not only world rulers, but the corroborating majority they govern are implicated. This means that these who are a part of this world and who uphold this political system, *regardless of their religious affiliation*, will suffer destruction.

The subject matter of Armageddon is gravely misinterpreted, but not only by extremists. Its significance is so rarely esteemed that a modern book or cyclopedia, more likely than not, will fail to make any application to it. Since Armageddon is to be fought on earth, which is shown by the assertion that the "earthly kings and their armies will be gathered together," and the expression "Har-Magedon" means "Mount of Megiddo," are we to assume that it would be fought at the location bearing that name?

Valley Plain of Megiddo

Clearly, Armageddon or Har-Magedon is symbolic as there has never been a mountain named Megiddo. However, the vision draws much of its significance from what transpired there. The hill city of Megiddo had been located to the southeast of Mount Carmel and some sixty miles northwest of Jerusalem. It was constructed on a tract of land over ten acres upon a mound known today as Tell el-Mutesellim. It rises nearly seventy feet above the valley plain below. Archaeology uncoverings reveal that the city had walls approximately fifteen feet thick and eleven feet in height. Megiddo was a royal city of the Canaanites, and its rulers had subjugated towns under its political influence (Joshua 17:11). The broad valley that the city towered over was called the "valley plain of Megiddo" (2 Chronicles 35:22).

Historically, decisive battles were fought in the region not only in Bible times, but also in secular history. The first assertion of Megiddo lists the city's king among the thirty-one that Judge Joshua defeated in his conquest of the Promised Land (Joshua 12:7, 8, 21, 24). When Joshua launched out against the enemy by surprise, "Yahweh went throwing them into confusion before Israel," resulting in a great slaughter at Gibeon. As they were fleeing, "God hurled great stones from the heavens upon them" and "there were more who died from the hailstones" (Joshua 10:1-15). This conquest was one of the most spectacular victories in all of human history. Significantly, a true "act of God" made it possible.

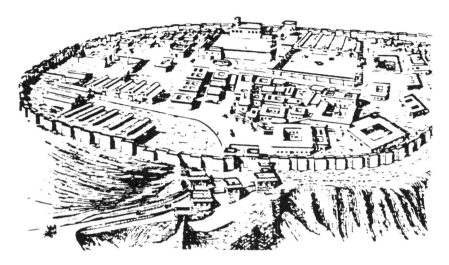

During an early period in the time of the judges, the Israelites had apostatized from the true worship and proceeded to select new gods. Because of this deplorable activity, Yahweh tolerated his people to suffer oppression under Jabin, king of Canaan. The conditions were so bad that the "caravans ceased" and the Israelite "travelers kept to the byways." Judges 5:6-8).

Eventually, they found themselves "by the waters of Megiddo," and militarily, the situation seemed hopeless. In comparison to the number of troops employed in modern warfare, the battle in the region of Megiddo was a small-scale event. Judge Barak had only ten thousand men and the prophetess Deborah. They were against forces without a "shield or spear to be seen" among them (Judges 5:8). Captain Sisera had, in addition to ground troops, nine hundred horse-drawn chariots, armed with scythes that could literally mow down a huge formation of foot soldiers.

In answer to their pleas for help, God sent his representative, Deborah, to march along with them. In the summertime, the Kishon River often becomes dry, and it was through this riverbed that Sisera and his army marched against Barak and his men on Mount Tabor. But before Barak and his men could establish contact with the enemy, God intervened and consequently weakened their forces.

Only the Creator could have produced a heavy cloudburst of rain at the exact psychological time, which brought about a flash flood in the Kishon River valley.

"Kings came, they fought
    It was then that the kings of Canaan fought
    In Taanach by the waters of Megiddo.
    No gain of silver did they take.
    From heaven did the stars fight,
    from their orbits they fought against Sisera.
    The torrents of Kishon washed them away
    and completely immobilized his forces"
(Judges 5:19-21).

Indisputably, the inspired words that Barak and Deborah sang at the close of their song apply as a prayer with reference to the coming war at Har-Magedon. They sang:

"So perish all thine enemies, O LORD! But thy friends be like the sun as he rises in his might" (Judges 5:31).

Some two years had passed since Joshua died. When the angel appeared to Judge Gideon, he was threshing wheat with a flail in the winepress to conceal it from predatory tyrants. His call to be a deliverer was put to the test by commands to destroy the altar of Baal.

After this, the Midianites, together with the Amalekites, encamped in the low plain of Jezreel. For fear of an invasion, they became a threat to Israel. Clothed by the spirit of God, Gideon blew a trumpet and was joined by Zebulun, Naphtali and even the reluctant Asher. Strengthened by a double sign from God, he reduced his army of 32,000 to a mere 300. The midnight surprise attack upon the 135,000 enemy troops was devastating. With 300 blasting trumpets, the smashing of 300 earthenware jars, the shouting of 300 powerful war cries, and at the same time lighting the sky with their 300 torches, threw the enemy into panic, and they "proceeded to set the sword of each one against the other in all the camp" (Judges 7:19-22). More importantly, the credit for the victory belonged to God.

Later, King David extracted the city from the Philistines. It thrived until another battle at Megiddo led to its capture by the Egyptian Shishak in the days of Jeroboam I. In time, King Jeroboam II reinstated it, but it was eventually seized by Assyrian Tiglath-Pileser III who named the entire area of northern Galilee the "Province of Megiddo."

Approaching modern times, there was Napoleon who handed the Turks a pungent defeat in 1739, and the British troops, under Field Marshall Allenby, defeated the Turkish forces through the Megiddo pass in 1918.

In light of the foregoing, Megiddo takes on a twofold meaning. First, a disastrous defeat for one side and an illustrious victory for the other side. Har-Magedon signifies that ultimate state that world affairs will come, the time in which the political rulers unitedly will apply force to make their will manifest and the time that God must respond with a countermeasure according to his design.

Secondly, these victories were made highly significant because they were not achieved by Israelite strength of arms alone. God fought in behalf of his people and with *natural forces,* rather than with man's tactical devices.

Logically, symbolic Armageddon can properly be related to the "war of the great day of God the Almighty." At Armageddon, God imposes upon his enemies a decisive quelling defeat that affects all nations and peoples.

Possessing a Scriptural viewpoint of what it really means will keep concerned persons from looking to the geographical location of ancient Megiddon in the land of Israel. Individuals will not be looking for a converging of all the armed forces of the nations there with the Republic of Israel as their target of attack. One will not be looking for a mass conversion of the Jews to accept Jesus Christ as the Messiah. The idea that Christians must line up with the natural Jews in order to survive is nonsensical. The Republic of Israel is not the issue, and this will become even more evident as the foremost adversary, Gog, makes his final ingress.

Gog of Magog

The kings of the earth are not heavenly minded. The gathering of the nations for the concluding battle cannot be interpreted as their direct challenge to God's spiritual forces. Naturally, they cannot literally fight the invisible kingdom, but they can attack those who visibly represent his kingdom here on earth.

A closer study of the expression, "Har-Magedon" helps us to discover who the forces are. The name Megiddo means "rendezvous or assembly of troops." Since Megiddo was in the land of Yahweh's people, the troops assembled today at this time of the end must be true praisers or Christians, although in the minority. The apostle Paul in his letter to the Ephesians asserted that "we have a wrestling against the wicked spirit forces in the heavenly places." Under Satan's authority, the nations will launch their attack against the troops already assembled out of all nations. It is this worldwide assault on God's people that he likens to the "touching of his eyeball" and that provokes the war of Armageddon (Zechariah 2:8).

If an attack upon an unwarlike, beneficent people was so significant that it was foretold over twenty-five centuries ago, it is more vital to consider the attacker and the cryptic name that was applied to his felonious character. For years, the perplexity of this designation has caused many to make application by straining the Scriptures to conform to their own preconception. Consenting with religion in general, Hal Lindsey, in his book, *The Late Great Planet Earth*,

232

erroneously pretends that *Magog* is "Russia," hence, asserting *Gog* to be "Russian leaders."

God apprises his prophet Ezekiel to shift his face toward Gog and to prophesy against him:

> "And the word of God continued to occur to me, saying: 'Son of man, set your face against Gog of the land of Magog, the head chieftain of Meshech and Tubal, and prophesy against him. And you must say, This is what the Sovereign Lord God has said: Here I am against you, O Gog, you head chieftain of Meshech and Tubal' " (Ezekiel 38:1-3).

The latest Biblical lexicographers suggest that "Gog" is a derivation from the Sumerian word gug meaning "darkness." This would agree with Christ Jesus' premise to the apostle Paul when he said, "I am sending you, to open their eyes, to turn them from darkness to light and from the authority of Satan to God" (Acts 26:17, 18). So all the related facts are attributed to Satan, the Devil as "Gog" and the "vicinity of the earth" of which he was cast as "Magog" [the decadent realm of the invisible component of Satan's world]. Magog was the name of one of Japheth's seven sons. His land of residence is believed to have been located geographically in northeastern Europe and Central Asia; however, this does not signify that the prophecy is making reference to the land of the Soviet Union. There are three strong reasons for this critique that would expel any such connotation.

First, as previously described, Satan's visible organization is illustrated by "a wild beast with ten horns [complete power] and seven heads [seven consecutive powers] and upon its horns, ten diadems" [complete number of dominating kings]. Russia became an extension of this political entity and eventually assumed the role of the king of the north as well as a constituent of the fabricated image of execution, the United Nations. Therefore, the land of the

Soviet Socialist Republics is but a cog in the massive political structure of Gog.

Secondly, Revelation 20:8 says that Gog of Magog is mentioned with a different time location from what Ezekiel's prophesied. In Ezekiel's vision, Magog is premillennial, whereas John envisioned Magog located at the end of the millennial reign of Christ, at which time the land of Russia would be nonexistent.

Finally, one must look at the relationship of lands and peoples to Gog from secular history. Some translations render Ezekiel 38:2 as "Gog, the Prince of Rosh," and unwarrantably reason that "Rosh" means Russia. However, it correctly signifies "head," which is only fitting to the "chief prince," "the great prince," or "the sovereign prince." Many translations identify with God's archenemy Satan, the Devil. The lands and peoples mentioned were materialistically involved with the king of Tyre, who also pictured God's adversary (Ezekiel 28:1, 2, 13-18). Hence, the regions denote the visible forces of Gog, making it a conglomerate army of "many peoples."

The Ultimate Battle

Accorded any amount of time, the nations would resume their course of destruction and leave the world in despair. God will not postpone his unavoidable intervention. He has his own appointed time to dispose of these incapable rulers whose prolongation would only tend to add further ruination and threaten the subsistence of all life forms.

What will set in motion the "Ultimate Battle?" The prophetic account respecting Gog and his forces, both invisible and visible, discloses that God will manipulate his enemy to dramatize an all-out assault upon his seemingly defensive people on earth. Then God's forces under the roaring Lion, Jesus Christ, will take them unexpectedly as recorded:

"Whenever it is that they are saying: 'Peace and security!' then sudden destruction is to be instantly upon them just as the pang of distress upon a pregnant woman; and they will by no means escape" (2 Thessalonians 5:3).

On October 24, 1985, the General Assembly of the United Nations solemnly announced that 1986 is the international "Year of Peace." It is highly improbable that the world will be any nearer to peace than it has been since the League of Nations was established in 1919. However, can Bible scholars presume that this eventful year will prove to be the fulfillment of Paul's words to the Thessalonians, or just an initial undertaking to that exterminating quotation? The precious little time that is left should be viewed with caution, but with a keen interest.

The day and hour of the execution approaches! By the use of "hooks in Satan's jaws," Yahweh escorts him and his throng down through the symbolic language of Ezekiel's prophecy (Ezekiel 38:4-6). Gog now positions himself for the final confrontation, his envisionary quest for domination already committed! The Sovereign One is prompted to crush Gog by means of "the Lion from the tribe of Judah," the Great Seed of his woman. A closer glimpse of the conflict unmasks a prevailing army under Christ Jesus:

"And out of his mouth there protrudes a sharp long sword, that he may strike the nations with it, and he will shepherd them with a rod of iron. He treads, too, the press of the wine of the anger of the wrath of God the Almighty" (Revelation 19:15).

The global winepress of God's infuriation will pulverize the political vine of the earth and the grapes of unpardonable atrocities they produced. Just as winemaking was a jovial occasion in Palestine, the treaders of the symbolic winepress will indubiously shout and sing as the roar is heard from heaven. Jeremiah emphasizes this controversy with the nations and affirms that:

> "The LORD roars from on high, from his holy dwelling he raises his voice; Mightily he roars over the range, a shout like that of vintagers over the grapes. To all who inhabit the earth to its very ends the uproar spreads; For the LORD has an indictment against the nations. He is to pass judgement upon all mankind; the godless shall be given to the sword" (Jeremiah 25:30, 31).

An interesting reality evolves as John further describes this arduous enemy and the results of their perversity. On one side of the battlement will be the political organizations on earth under Gog's constraint. This embraces the kings of the earth and all their subservient forces. Ironically, on the opposite side of the visionary fortification no earthly fighting troops are seen with defensive armament. Logically, this is sound because according to prophecy, it is the invisible armies in heaven that will wage the conflict against the political establishment. The inspired prognosis is indicative:

> "Then I saw the beast and the kings of the earth and their armies gathered together to make war against the rider on the horse and his army. But the beast was captured, and with him the false prophet who had performed the miraculous signs on his behalf. With these signs he had deluded those who had received the mark of the beast and worshiped his image" (Revelation 19:19, 20).

Regressing to the chapter, "Seven Heads of Predominance," you will recall that the wild beast [United Nations] received its power, throne and great authority from the dragon [Satan]. The false prophet [Anglo-American power] inherently gets authority in their original connection with the symbolic seventh head of the political wild beast (Revelation 13:1, 2, 11-15).

During the day the lion roars, the "false prophet" will establish his falsehood, having pointed the populus to the "image of the beast" [United Nations] as the world's last hope of peace. This, in effect, is a denial of the Kingdom of God and of his "Prince of Peace."

Here is where wisdom comes in, and the all important key that is revealed for our edification. The "wild beast" and the "false prophet" will be symbolically "captured alive," while tempting to desolate the true followers of the established Kingdom. God now will demand back the shed blood that was apparent throughout all human history. Although desperately trying to escape from their confinement, they will be unable to "tear their bands apart or cast their cords away" (Psalms 2:1-4).

The written word avows that these *political organizations* will be entirely "burned up" or *cease to be*; however, the kings of the earth, their armies, and the corroborating population *will remain*. All political authority, alliances, and uniformity will be dilapidated. It will be a short period of time when no restraint will be present, thus resulting in bewilderment and anarchy. "On that day there shall be among them a great tumult from the LORD: every man shall seize the hand of his neighbor, and the hand of each shall be raised against that of his neighbor" (Zechariah 14:13). Jesus reassures his followers by asserting:

> "In fact, unless those days were cut short, no flesh would be saved; but on account of the chosen ones, those days will be cut short" (Matthew 24:22).

What cosmic or other forces God will utilize in destroying the ungodly would only be conjectural; however, Job dramatizes his storehouse:

> "Have you entered into the storehouse of the snow,

or do you see even the storehouses of the hail, which I have kept back for the time of distress, for the day of fight and war? Can you raise your voice even to the cloud, so that a heaving mass of water itself may cover you? Can you send forth lightnings that they may go and say to you, 'Here we are!' " (Job 38:22, 23, 34, 35).

The inevitable end of civilization as we know it will be a startling surprise to the world: the deflation of government and direction, terrifying upheavals of the earth, cloudbursts causing flash floods as never before, landslides of immeasurable movement, electrical storms permeating the environment with cindery decadence, rain of corrosive liquid fire, and unnerved fear on the land, in the air and on the seas. The emanation of the sun and the atmosphere working together could produce and discharge more energy than science can by detonating one hundred nuclear bombs. Those who may survive in the encounter against his fellow man will ultimately be executed through supernatural means by the spiritual forces of God's King of kings. None of them will evade the judgement of the Lion.

The degree of the slaughter may be determined by the final count of the enemy destroyed. The wooden fragments of the blood-stained weapons will be so abundant "that they will have to light fires seven years. And they will not carry sticks of wood from the field, nor will they gather firewood out of the forests, for with the armor they will light fires" (Ezekiel 39:9, 10).

The affirming prophecy discloses that those decimated at Armageddon "will certainly come to be in that day from one end of the earth to the other end of the earth. They will not be wailed, neither will they be gathered up or buried. As manure on the ground they will become" (Jeremiah 25:33). Even the once terrified birds and beasts of the field will share in the benefits of the victory. The "fleshly parts of the kings and military commanders and strong men and

238

horses and those seated on them" are shown as being left as food for the carrion-eating birds of the heavens. However, the burial of the bones for cleansing the land will not symbolize a resurrection hope. The valley will be called "The Valley of Gog's Mob," and the symbolic city nearby will be known as "Hamonah," [meaning mob] as a memorial of God's triumphant day.

The nations of the earth are only consenting victims. The imperceptible wicked forces in the realm of Magog are the provokers; therefore, they will not elude the pernicious release of God's fury. John envisions the unworldly seizure:

> "And I saw an angel coming down out of heaven with the key of the abyss and a great chain in his hand. And he seized the dragon, the original serpent, who is the Devil and Satan, and bound him for a thousand years. And he hurled him into the abyss and shut it and sealed it over him, that he might not mislead the nations any more until the thousand years were ended. After these things he must be let loose for a little while" (Revelation 20:1-3).

After all the visible elements of Satan have been destroyed, then the Lion, Jesus Christ, will take Gog and his demon hoard and cast them into the abyss of death. There they will remain for one thousand years to be loosed briefly to test mankind before their final unending destruction. With their incarceration, the war of Armageddon ends.

Reconversion

After God's heavenly government cleanses this earth of those who obstinately reject his requisite for life, a thousand-year-long program will go into effect to conduct all those living to a state of human perfection.

Since the global deluge was a type of Har-Magedon, it is reasonable that the experience Noah and his family shared should also be a type. So those Christians who survive the great tribulation at Armageddon will have the same privilege of subduing the land and thereby extending a paradisiac estate to the four corners of the earth. They will accomplish this in absolute peace with God, peace with one another, and peace with the lower, subservient creatures. The Psalmist relates that "the righteous themselves will possess the earth, and they will reside forever upon it" (Psalm 37:29).

God's Kingdom rule will eradicate competition. Since only one government will dominate, there is logically to be only one system of economics. Work under this ideal arrangement will enable one to see the direct results of his labor.

Reflect on man's existence now and perhaps, the few years that are remaining. Are capabilities being utilized to the greatest measure possible? How many deeds of accomplishment could one fulfill if there was only allowable time and needed assets available?

It would be unsound for imperfect man to reason that such eternal knowledge would eventually come to a standstill because everything would have been achieved. However, today there is no way to fathom the depths of a supernatural love. "Eye has not seen and ear has not heard, nor has it so much as been conceived in the heart of man the good things God has prepared for those who love him" (I Corinthians 2:9).

Perhaps individuals would display some talent in music, painting or sculpturing. What infinitesimal performance could one realize after one or two thousand years? There are mechanics, woodworking, architecture and designing, or possibly the higher mental development of mathematics or astronomy. Could it be conceived that man's capabilities would be limited?

Possibly some would like to adopt the agronomics of specific plants, or the endogamy of animals, birds or fish. Today, scientists believe there are more than 350,000 species of plants, but no one knows for certain. Some of the smallest plants, called diatoms, can be seen only through a microscope. A drop of water may contain some 500 diatoms.

Zoologists and entomologists have described and named about one million kinds of animals. Of these, more than 800,000 are insects. They disclose an average of 8,000 new kinds of insects every year. They believe there may be nearly ten million kinds still unknown.

Bacteria are among the smallest of cells. Some believe that they are neither plants nor animals but a separate group called protista. They can be found almost everywhere. The air we breathe may contain more than 100 microorganisms per cubic foot.

There is little danger of exhausting the ability to mature. One can find true pleasure by feeling gentle breezes, hearing the sounds of water beating against the shore, seeing an intermittent stream flowing over a variety of polished stones, hearing the chirping of birds, and seeing clear lakes or plunging waterfalls. Towering mountains and the scent of an array of colored blossoms are but a few of the rich and rewarding blessings that one can commit to memory and relate beneficially. It will likewise allow mankind endless opportunities to express love and to experience the love of others.

Conclusion

The reign of one thousand years will facilitate the righteous subjects to grow progressively young and strong until they attain perfection of health in mind and body. They will be set completely free from the bondage of sin and death inherited from the first human creation (Revelation 21:4).

Into this earthly pleasance will also be the privilege of welcoming thousands of millions of resurrected dead. What an exquisite future is soon to be relished by mankind! What a change this earth is to undergo and "the former things will pass away."

The day the lion roars will be a war that will end all wars. Only by it will the war-minded and war-rousing agitators of all human society be expunged forever. Men proned to righteousness will need not fear at the apprehension of such a war of universal proportions. Ample security will be provided as God's inspired word directs his servants to "Go, my people, enter into your interior rooms, and shut your doors behind you. Hide yourself for but a moment until the denunciation passes over" (Isaiah 26:20).

Seemingly, *within the critical next ten years*, all mankind stands in danger of violently destroying itself by its own machinations. What is happening throughout the world today is in fulfillment of Bible prophecy and indicates that those living will see the final destruction. Awaking now to the real state of affairs will see God bring to life again his aggressive act of olden times.

References

A History of Christianity by Kenneth Latourette (Harper & Brothers of New York)

Medieval History by Norman Cantor (Macmillan Publishing Co. Inc.)

Origin and Evolution of Religion by E. Washburn Hopkins (Yale University Press)

A Survey of European Civilization by Geoffrey Bruun (Houghton Mifflin Co.)

Heroes and Heretics by Barrows Dunham (Alfred A. Kropf, Inc.)

Study to the Holy Scripture by Charles Briggs (Baker Book House)

Greece by J. A. McClymont (A & C Black)

Hellenism by Norman Bentich (The Jewish Publication Society of America)

Erasmus by John Paynes (John Knox Press)

The Origin of Species by Charles Darwin (The Modern Library)

Tertullian and Minucius Felix translated by T. R. Glover (Harvard University Press)

Plato: The Republic translated by Benjamin Jowett (The Heritage Press)

The Story of Civilization by Will Durant (Simon and Schuster)

The Outline of History by H. G. Wells (Garden City Books)

Beacon Lights of History by John Lord (Fords, Howard and Hulbert)

A History of the World by Starr, Nowell, Lyon, Stearns and Hamerow (Rand McNally & Co.)

World Civilizations by Burns and Ralph (W. W. Norton & Co., Inc.)

The City of God by Saint Augustine (The Modern Library)

In the Pillory by John Bond (The Fellowship Forum)

Civilization Past and Present by Wallbank and Taylor Scott, Foresman and Company)

A History of Germany by William Carr (St. Martin's Press)

The Protestant Reformation by Lewis Spitz (Prentice-Hall, Inc.)

The March of Civilization by Jesse Wrench (Charles Scribner's Sons)

History of the World by J. N. Larned (World Syndicate Co., Inc.)

Josephus Complete Works translated by William Whiston (Kregel Publications)

The Two Babylons by Alexander Hislop (Loizeaux Brothers)

Encyclopaedia Britannica, 1968 Edition

World Book Encyclopedia, 1980 Edition

A History of Europe by H. A. Fisher (Houghton Mifflin Co.)

Americas Rise to World Power by Foster Dulles (Harper and Row)

World Since 1914 by Landman and Wender (Barnes and Noble)

Bible Translations

American Standard Version (1901)
American Revised Standard (1952)
Jerusalem Bible (1966)
New American Bible (1970)
New English Bible (1961)
Bible in Living English by Byington (1972)
The Bible by James Moffatt (1954)
The Holy Bible by Knox (1950)
The Catholic Douay (4th Edition)
An American Translation by Goodspeed (1933)
The King James Version (8th Edition)
Holy Scriptures According to Masoretic Text (1955)
The New World Translation (1981)
The NIV Triglott Old Testament (1981)
Emphasized Bible by Rotherham (1981)
Young's Literal Translation (1898)
The Emphatic Diaglott (1942)
Interlinear Translation by Westcott and Hort (1969)
The New International Version (1978)
Catholic Confraternity Version (1941)
Holy Bible from Ancient Eastern Manuscripts (1951)
The Modern Reader's Bible (1907)
The Authentic New Testament (1958)
The New Testament by Sharpe (1859)
The New Testament in Modern Speech by Weymouth (1902)
The Syriac Peshitta
Greek Septaugint Version (LXX)
Sagrada Biblia (1944)